Algerian
WHITE

Algerian WHITE

A NARRATIVE

Assia Djebar

TRANSLATED FROM THE FRENCH
BY DAVID KELLEY AND
MARJOLIJN DE JAGER

Seven Stories Press
New York / London / Sydney / Toronto

Seven Stories Press
140 Watts Street
New York, NY 10013
http://www.sevenstories.com

In Canada:
Hushion House, 36 Northline Road, Toronto, Ontario M4B 3E2, Canada

In the U.K.:
Turnaround Publisher Services Ltd., Unit 3, Olympia Trading Estate, Coburg Road, Wood Green, London N22 6TZ U.K.

Library of Congress Cataloging-in-Publication Data

Djebar, Assia, 1936-
    [Blanc de l'Algérie. English.]
    Algerian white / Assia Djebar
    p. cm.
    ISBN 1-58322-050-X; 1-58322-516-1 pbk
1. Algeria—History—Revolution, 1954-1962. 2. Authors, Algerian—20th century. 3. Politics and literature—Algeria. 4. Islam and politics—Algeria—History—20th century. I. Title.

DT295 .D5413 2001
965'046—dc21

00-051014

9 8 7 6 5 4 3 2 1

Book design by Cindy LaBreacht

Printed in the U.S.A.

*In memory of three friends
who are gone:*

MAHFOUD BOUCEBI

M'HAMED BOUKHOBZA

ABDELKADER ALLOULA

Contents

1
The Language
of the Dead

"Hurry up and die, then you
will speak as ancestors…"

Kateb Yacine
L'Oeuvre en fragments

"If I had the power to give voice to our solitude and anguish,
it would be in that voice that I would speak to you now."

Albert Camus,
Algiers (lecture, January 22, 1956)

I wanted, in this account, to respond to an immediate demand of memory: the death of close friends (a sociologist, a psychiatrist and a dramatist); to recount a few flashes of an old friendship, but also to describe, in each case, the day of the assassination and that of the funeral—what each of these three intellectuals represented, in his singularity and his authenticity, for those close to him, for his town of origin, his tribe.

Then the desire was instilled in me to unroll a procession: that of the writers of Algeria, over at least one generation, caught at the approach of death—whether it be by accident, illness or, in the case of the most recent ones, by murder.

I do not wish to polemecize; nor do I want to practice the exercise of literary lament. As simply as possible (and in some cases after making inquiries of a few people close to them) I re-establish an account of the days—with sometimes innocent signs, presages—the days leading up to the death.

And yet *Algerian White* is not an account of death on the march in Algeria. Gradually, in the course of this procession, intercut with flashbacks to the war of yesterday, an irresistible search for a liturgy emerges, materializing through the pen over a little more than thirty years, marking a score of deaths of men and women.

Regrouping, reassembling, then dispersing around these writers definitively resting (some while their novel or some article or another was still unfinished, the ink not quite dry), the survivors, their readers and friends. "Those of their family"—spiritually more than by blood—

sometimes went in for traditional practices (particularly religious ones) at the moment of burial; but some—as for example at the funeral of Kateb Yacine, in November 1989—insisted on declaiming slogans: associations of young Berbers, feminist groups. And there was just as much singing of the national anthem of independence: several different styles faced each other at the side of open graves.

For me, sustained as I am by the search for a scrupulously faithful account, I have been brought to note that new rituals were in the coming into being: the writer once dead, his texts not yet reopened, it is around his buried body that several different Algerias are being sketched out...

A nation seeking its own ceremonial, in different forms, but from cemetery to cemetery, because, first of all, the writer has been offered as propitiatory victim: strange and despairing discovery!

THE LANGUAGE OF THE DEAD

Midway on our life's journey,
I found myself in the middle of a dark wood

DANTE
The Divine Comedy, Hell I, 1, 1-2.

I

Those dear disappeared: they speak to me. All three; each of the
three.

My friends spoke to me in French, in the past; each of the three,
in fact, conversed with me in a foreign language; through humility,
or austerity. Except for Kader, who with tempered exuberance—at
least after the first year of a friendship which gradually became familiar and then familial—would forget himself so far as to improvise in
his Arabic with the accent of Oran, recounting anecdotes which he
would punctuate with "ouah, ouah"—the "oui" Moroccan style—
over which I sometimes teased him. And yet I would reply to him, as
to the two others, in French: all else failing, out of neutrality.

(On the few occasions, it seems to me, where I must have started
spontaneously a sentence in my local urban dialect, I knew immedi-

15

ately that I appeared precious—to Kader—even perhaps outdated, and that because of the softness of the dental consonants in the accent of the women from the place where I was brought up—so quickly went back to the impersonality of French. In a second, by the flash of his gaze, I understood: speaking in Arabic together, we were becoming, excessively so, I an old-fashioned *bourgeoise* and he a crude rough village lad!... No, we just seemed different by suddenly perceived atavisms in the variations of our mother tongue!)

As though the unspoken that necessarily carried with it a precautionary friendship to express itself between a man and a woman of my land, as though the pulsion towards silence, that dark undercurrent constantly attempting to undermine the simplest of our communications, the language of our ancestors, ready to rise up, was there to be choked on.

<u>2</u>

So, in the old days, I mean in life, we would chat—each of these three friends and myself, in French—but this cover would spread itself over another, shadowy, phreatic, the invisible which could always surge into view.

And now?

Now, each of those three dear disappeared and myself, at irregular intervals, all speak in French. This language flows, is woven or tangled, but never masked, nor is the veiled walker—on taking the place of another; no, it unfurls among us, truly itself, in its own right. Belatedly, our speech becomes so simple!

And why do I call them "disappeared" only to attenuate the "dear" which is rooted in a tenderness, a limpidity purely Arab? Have they really disappeared? No, I stubbornly refuse the evidence; I refuse right up to the end, to the very end of this ramble, of this remembrance of the "afterwards," of what I learned about them in that afterwards... Of course, I should be convinced, so often do I fix on— sometimes in full daylight, in the midst of some trite activity with others, people of the sun, fit and well—sometimes I fix on the image of the last moment: when they fell one after the other, slaughtered, one upright, walking tall as he was, his head holed in an instant, the second and the third, chest lacerated, ripped with the knife, and they surround him and draw blood, and...

I am there, amidst the survivors, sometimes in the white harshness of the midday sun, on a Parisian boulevard, sometimes in a town where I arrived two hours earlier, speaking or listening, with a single gulp taking in the faces, the houses, the brick facades, the brilliance of the sun—and, then the final still shots that rip the air in slow motion, sound severed, I feel suddenly lost in the midst of the others.... It's more than a year in the case of Kader, almost two for M'Hamed and Kader, that I am haunted by them in full daylight, it matters not where but elsewhere, far from the earth where they thought to bury them.... Did they bury them? One after the other? With speeches, harangues, chants, photographers, with...? Do they really sleep over there?

Fortunately they speak to me often, these "dear ones." That *cher* that I shall from now onwards be able to say to them, with no false modesty, in Arabic, in my Arabic, with its flattened out dentals. They never disappeared. They are there; they sometimes come close to me, together or separately...Whispering shadows.

3

Thus there came to light, in a light, gray by its very glitter, the noise of language, their language, the language of all three of them, each in turn and all together, with me too: a French with neither nerves nor veins, nor even memories, a French both abstract and carnal, warm in its consonances. "Their" French, the French of my friends—so they disappeared, will I finally end up knowing it, believing it—whereas, freed from the shroud of the past, the French of the old days now begins to be generated within us, between us, transformed into a language of the dead.

Henceforth they speak to me, those close to me, my allies, certainly not in the same way as the ancestors whom, in childhood or in our jolty adolescence, we each were called upon, ardently or peevishly—in my case my confrontational dialogues with the possessive grandmother who was neither forgetful nor forgotten. My friends come to me, I have never called them, and of course they should have stayed in my company, steadfastly present as in the past, reserved, tight-tongued; and yet they hurried off, went before me, over there, so far away.... But now, they speak to me, in volumes.

Nevertheless, they went before me: sometimes their gait sways on the horizon, in the midst of a meadow or in a sharp ray of sunlight.

4

Sometimes they come and sit above my bed in a circle, like saints in naive pictures, no halo around their heads—sometimes solitary silhouettes, one rather than the other, whispering some memory or another, giving the once suspended or uncertain meaning back to it, sometimes in that conversation which is tangled and braided and palpitating—fringing my fore dawn exit from sleep—I no longer know who is speaking—of me or the person approaching; I no longer know who is the phantom—myself, in turn, beginning to float horizontally in the ether, ears gaping, eyelids hardly closed, and smile peaceful in the half-light—or the first among them, with his usual look,

M'Hamed, if really it's him I pick out from his stiffness, his bony brown face, standing upright, in the same old suit as before, a bit tight on him, he sways, stands up straight, a hint of a smile above his slim brown moustache—I'm no longer sure whether this is happening as it did twenty years ago in his office, both of us absorbed in the sociological commentary I was setting out, me presenting the finished inquiry, he letting slip that all means ("all technical and human means," in the pompous terminology of French bureaucracy) had been put in service, but perhaps not so far back, perhaps just a few months before he went away, that we were three (or rather we speak now as we did when we were three), the third, our common friend, we are sitting in my place, in the little suburban house, and the two of us are speaking seriously, but the common friend is making jokes, rubbing up against M'Hamed's stiffness and I lower my eyes—that is what we recall, the two of us, in that new language which has wiped away our mutual reticence, the holding back of other times.

5

I am in California; I am sleeping, or rather I can't sleep at my normal times: so, the friend has crossed the Atlantic, then floated over the whole of the American West, so that at this hour, neither of night nor day, he can begin to let me glimpse, by a simple hint, why before, in the suburban house, he had smiled indulgently before the common friend, our intercessor into the realm of bizarre humor, he so impatient, the joker.... M'Hamed speaks to me of these little details, almost details of family life: and we murmur, both of us, there in that distant place.

I've already said that we speak French. Not in the old way. Not by cautiousness, nor by convention, to hide our imperceptible embarrassment, our common stiffness. There, on American soil, our

French from before the dawn flows just as simply, after all, as the mother tongue we share.

So, dear friends, before, did we find it so difficult to have an open dialogue? Our French was on parade, a ceremonial uniform...

6

Suddenly overwhelmed by unhinging doubt or some regret—just before the wrinkles of dawn, within the waters of a twilight time of somber stream—: from now on, with you, what have I acquired since the break, since what was irreparable? Shall I at last be able to weep? Not weep for you, you are still with me, you even mount the guard for me, I know that, not weep for you, no. (*That would mean that I aspire to a return, a return to that place, in the midst of the gushing blood, the faces of young killers resurging, a second, in the eye of the storm, I could but free myself from living there, in your wake take flight!*)

Deplore rather what was impossible in yesterday's dialogue between us, the invisible knot which made our intermingled speech slip aside, the veil-shroud which made me draw back my impulses within myself in front of each of you—and my laughter could only be perceived as a smile, my rising joy would dam itself up to seem like a hesitation in saying yes—except once, with Kader.

7

To him I went that day toward the end of winter—where there breathes a white diaphanous light, almost unreal, lengthening those dense yet almost weightless days.... I'd taken the plane, my other friends leaving for Carthage, or Sidi-Bou-Said: we had been working well together, was I too to be tempted by those three days off? But suddenly, on the telephone, I was talking to Kader: "You remember:

you promised to show me the whole of Oran! All of it! Shall I come?"

I never told him that I was about to give up a group escapade in Tunis and Carthage—three or four joyous comrades rushing off to others waiting for them.

We all went together to the airport; I leaving them to go in the opposite direction. I took off for Oran (in the previous weeks he had been coming regularly from
Algiers to Tipasa, to share our evenings). I took off for Kadar's Oran, the city and its deepest depths, which he had sketched out for me...

I still used the formal *vous* with him. Still no familiarity between us. This time something of a family occasion: three sisters, as in the theater, but without the melancholy; one of them, almost his twin (with wide eyes, a tall and harmonious silhouette, above all a contained energy in every gesture towards others, towards people). Time to have lunch, time for a few stifled laughs; other young girls turned up. But we left, the two of us, for the discovery that made me impatient, that I was waiting for: the town.

Up above, the peak of Murdjadjo, below, a great distance. The seas of el-Kabir and Cape Falcon, to the East the Bay of Oran, the port and its docks.... As we were discovering the pines of the Ravine of Planters (on the other end Bordj el-Ahmar, just glimpsed: "At the top, you can see the *fort des Cigognes*"), then, driving by car to the center ("That used to be the Lycée Lamoricière," and me proud of myself: "The two stone lions, work of the sculptor Cain!"), and as we drove around the town, splattered with cries and laughter, full of youths (oh, the youths of Oran, everywhere, leaning against a wall, on the vertical, in the sun, at every street corner, watching, laughing, cautious!), our tour was gradually fed by Kader's memories.

I nagged him: "Tell me! Show me the secret places! I want to see the underground places, you remember we once talked of the persecution of the trade-unionists, particularly in Oran!" "My longtime friend, my brother, a pity he is gone this time, for three months! We could have had dinner in a cheap restaurant, over there, you see! Perhaps, at the end of the evening, he would have answered your questions!..." And we walked up and down the quay; then a little later the Promenade of Letang. ("Oh, I remembered. I had seen it on several postcards, with the elegant *pieds-noirs* of the turn of the century, beneath the plane and bellòmbra trees!... You see, I recognize your town.) He was laughing at my voracious desire to know the places, a desire to drink in their history, their memory. I never stopped: "At least show me the cafes where the tough guys hang out!" And after some hesitation, in a lower tone: "And I know that you're friendly with licentious singers!"

And so we went round that day, sometimes hurrying, and sometimes with a silent slowness. Late, I dropped with tiredness at the door of the woman doctor friend who was putting me up.

<u>8</u>

Am I talking to you about this now? I relive that parenthesis in Oran, now I use the familiar "tu" with you, Kader, part of my family, seeing once more the white light of that day which seemed so long, the last flights of the migrating swallows invading, then deserting in a flash, or by multiplied flutterings, the plane trees in the colonial avenue. Is it you, now at the window, in that gray semi-dawn which reminds me of the washed-out filtered light of that day of the past, I admit to you only now the fatigue of that evening at my friend's house, a friend who knew you, you hadn't yet got married again, you hadn't yet had your youngest daughter.

You must often have unveiled for others the naked, tumultuous and impulsive, raucous, mocking town.

I can admit it now: while you stayed so serious in my presence (not in a group, where your humor, your joviality, your taste for anecdotes quickly took over—perhaps then my shyness, which looked like calm and coldness intimidated you in your turn?), so in that escapade of the end of a white winter, I lifted my head towards you walking by my side, and I saw acutely how far, speaking of your town as of a lover—your face changed, a smile broadened it, the shine in your eyes gave it color, the gestures of your arms, of the body, still mastered—but your face, above all your voice, I said to myself (and I say it again in my Californian room, amidst the waves of sleep): of course he speaks to me in French, yet his language suddenly starts out on a caper, takes on wings, begins to slide.... So, his French is the French of Oran; not because of the *pied-noir* accent; rather by its vivacity, the concentration of life which quivers in his speech!"

The next day, in the huge round apartment, the three sisters, friends, one or two cousins from Tlemcen, all around you like a traditional audience, myself coming back for the family feast, I looked at you amidst your own people and in your maternal language: you sang, made rhythms with your hands, everyone in turn told an anecdote, most often some chronicle from the street, the market, the quarter; we laughed and ate, myself squatting between the sister who looks so like you and the silent younger sister, myself catching a surprise glimpse of the quotidian theater of your life, you its hearth and its secret fire...

Someone asked me:

"You don't know their mother?"

"No, not yet."

And now, it is as though you are leaning at the half-open window sill, both of us mingling these memories; in French I describe to you the warmth of your language of the West, neither that of the city

enclosed within itself like the dialect I speak, nor a real rustic crudi-
ty, somewhere in between, a cross-breed of all possible influences,
retaining something of the vast horizon of the high plateaux. I
remind you of the scansion of your rhythms and your songs.

Someone else asked me again:

"You'll come again at midnight, the mother will be there, with
her sister from whom you can't keep her apart, and the girls will
dance, for her pleasure, for her joy!... and you?

"I'll dance too!" I said, looking sideways at Kader who was bringing in the food. "The paterfamilias, you are the paterfamilias of the
whole tribe," I said, allowing myself to be served.

Why do I talk to you, here, outside San Francisco, about my first
days in Oran with you? You keep close; I don't see you, I perceive you:
the window stays half open. The mist will slowly evaporate; so then
I'll show you a little bit of the depths of the bay.... But we are talking
about Oran: you are reminding me of the tale you told me of
Cheikha Remiti, already surrounded by her bodyguards.

You are laughing. Amidst your friends, in the Oran evening, you
make them hum the litanies of *la Cheikha*. Now, almost astride the
windowsill—as though, with the mist, you were about to dissipate as
well—you murmur or hum: "*La Cheikha*, do you remember her that
year?"

"Yes, of course, it was you who told me, during those days in Oran,
who told me of the pilgrimage, the first pilgrimage, from *la Cheikha* to
Mecca. Then to convince her that to sing wine, love, pleasure between
two people, remained allowable: it was hardly easy; impossible!"

In the bubbling atmosphere of the feast, one of the sisters whis-
pered to me that "only Kader, with patience and with passion, could

influence the priestess of *rai*, and get her to come back to her estranged fans."

The third day, you set off early for the capital, urgently called, you told me, by the high administration of the theater. I took the last evening plane, and, with an Algerian friend, you came to meet me at the airport.

That same year we walked so often in Algiers, without the perfect pearled complicity of those three days in Oran, with all their racket—that double vision of your town, as though it were turning upside down beneath our eyes: on its heights we looked down at our feet to its tumult, but passing before its mausoleums of saints or its low–life cafes, we felt its secrets more closely, its memory still tied up. And you would talk! There remains for me, in these spaces, the briskness of your verb, in each of the two languages, just the accent and its vivacity making the bridge between the two. I now know, and say it to you on American earth: never have I seen you so happy! I was listening to your inner rhythm...

<u>2</u>

I am almost falling asleep. You are silent; soon a bit of San Francisco Bay will appear on an edge of the horizon.

You are silent: daylight comes, will you go back, if only to protect with our invisible gaze, your last child: I beg you to come back the following night, sleepily, I insist, but gently.

Before (these memories go back ten years or more) I seemed to you, I'm not sure how, either timid or intimidating, laughing at anything, but reserved (it was in fact you who were the most reserved, sometimes even stiff and starchy), I certainly wasn't soft or sweet. No. I was hiding, by caution, my propensity to dream on the other side, on the other side of the sun, eyes open.

No, even in this new dawn in which you return, in which we take a taste for this surprising closeness, I won't tell you everything. (Besides we have all our time, truly.) You see, I rediscover your silent laughter, which makes your breast shudder, which vibrates within you.

From my bed, so leaning, I do not turn my head towards you: I know you in your habitual stance, well, the habitual stance of that period. You, peaceful, at ease, and your arm bent, hand hidden under your jacket, between jacket and pullover; a Napoleonic gesture. You often have this stance, when... When you were listening in that way, I thought of you as being older, more knowledgeable than you were. Reassuring too, but that was something that everyone noticed at first sight. I confess it to you now, almost in a tone of amusement: in this milieu of recognized or young actors, of wannabe actresses, looking like good and quiet students, sometimes made-up matrons, previously celebrated in traditional circles as variety stars, or singers of classical Andalusian music in Algiers or Oran, I say to you with tender indulgence: "You comforted the anguished, you exalted the slightest glows of enthusiasm, you played all the roles you didn't want on stage for yourself: the unruffled father, the friend and confidant, the discreet and altruistic guide, the "good roles" therefore, those bearing the burden of souls!

"But you remind me, you remind me of so many lost days!" replies Kader sadly (his voice reaching me hollowly, having lost its scintillating vibration). "We are so far from that time: ten years or more. Time's gone by."

"Not only time," I think to reply, when, awakened all at once, seated suddenly on the bed, I'm not sure how, lighting the lamp without reason, I see myself, in the room, invaded by the first glimmers of murky daylight coming through the windows. Empty, the room.

Bitter, I lie back down: "It isn't only time that's gone by, Kader. Life, too, life too has passed."

I was engaged in a monologue.

That morning I couldn't get back to sleep.

10

Three days passed. No more visitors. Whole mornings I plunged myself into my work: I was preparing my lecture on the work–in–progress in *The First Man* by Camus. I am trying to reconstruct, by soundings of the text and his notes, by verification of biographical details, the last fortnight of the life of the writer from Algiers:

"In *The First Man* Camus appears to us in an unaffected way, that is, in his haste and his anguish you can guess at. He has just left his house in Lourmarin, where for weeks he had been immersed in the isolation and effervescence of this last piece of writing; the next day, on a far-flung country road, he lay there on the road, among the skid marks of his friend and publisher's car: so, in those first days of 1960, Camus ran, in a single movement, within his text and towards death...

"Yes, death is a hatchet, and it left the shadow of its blade, of its blow, of its sagging towards the ground, in the very text. Yes, in this novel there is, on the one hand the accomplished work, and at the same time what is like a slow surging, imperceptibly half-opening up, in spite of the vacillating absence and the reflection of a close wound: the text shows us its flank; within its grain, you feel a flickering hesitation of light as well as an intensification of vitality."

So, the third day, my lecture at Berkeley. I read several pages of that talk which tries to stretch the last burst of Camus's enthusiasm to its limit. And then I improvise: on Camus's maternal non-language. His mother, almost dumb, remains seated eternally by the window (like my maternal aunt, so sweet, residing in Belcourt, who at this very moment is intoning, in sorrow or patience, scraps of verses of the Koran).

Hours after that lecture, I understood that I had spent a long time justifying, as an Algerian woman, never having paid any serious attention to Camus, as if not knowing that this time I was going to the other end of the earth, as though by duty, in spite of myself, to meet him, in this work in progress, which marks a renewal of his novelistic art.

Hours later, going to bed in the same room, those last nights, deserted by my shadows, I had a vague understanding of why I had been attracted to the last written words of a writer, at a moment when he was running towards his death. To his mother, who died six months after him in Belcourt, and yet still waiting at her window.

II

Before dawn the following day, they woke me up, the three of them, sitting cross-legged, a bit as if they were in a Persian miniature: the three of them (I don't even know if they knew each other, if they had met in the past), together without prompting each other, they smiled tenderly at me. Didn't speak. Seemed pleased with the efforts I'd made, the work I had done over the past three days; having guessed before I did the reasons for my stubborn digging into a literary text.

The evening before I had walked around the Italian quarter of San Francisco with an Arab student and two young Americans who spoke a literary Arabic full of elegance, of beauty, thanks to a long stay in Egypt.

I really would like you to comment on that, you, my friends; I rediscover a nostalgia for that mother tongue in which I do not write, a language flashing before me like a fugitive in a dress studded with diamonds of poetry!...

"Let's go off to Egypt together! Let's carry on our conversations there on the banks of the Nile, and so in our rediscovered language let's make gleam in turn its feminine dream, its rampant masculine roughness!"

Having found you once more my friends, I am ready—in spite of my tendency to laziness, my nonchalance—to go off, thus haunted by you, to Egypt, of course, to China, to the end of the world.... They vanish, or rather so I think. Suddenly Mahfoud explodes:

"When I'm in a consultation, I speak with my patients in the language they speak themselves!...Knowing what language reflects, its emotive power—is that not to be at the very center of change? A significant anecdote: once I had a fifty–year–old man who talked to me at length in classic Arabic of rare quality.

"He neither wanted to speak to me in French—which he spoke as well as I do—nor in a dialect of Arabic—not even in Berber. I didn't say anything: he was falling into a depressive state, with a neurosis that was easy to perceive. I finished up by interrupting him; I advised he seek a psychotherapist; my appointment book was full for the next six months. I tried to recommend a colleague: I pointed out that I didn't know anyone capable of treating him in his literary Arabic.

"He suddenly seemed to have his back to the wall. He insisted, sometimes in French—an impeccable French in fact—sometimes in a common Arabic dialect. We finished by finding a therapist. As I accompanied him to the door, I couldn't help giving him advice:

"Be simply Algerian! Be yourself—and I was thinking privately that half his therapy would be done!"

Mahfoud's voice suddenly seems to become distant—or is it me who's getting drowsy—and then I jump: Mahfoud has just laughed, a powerful laugh, slightly sharp toward the end, in any case an irrepressible laugh, and I hear him finish, as a farewell, as though for an audience of absent people:

"Of course I recognize that over there I'm the pain in the ass of psychiatry!"

From then on he seems to be alone. I can hear him soliloquize. I know his speech: he will never learn Arabic—literary Arabic that is—perhaps Berber, the most ancient language, which his grandparents used as their only means of speech. He carries on for ages, as in a lecture on Algerian soil. He polemicizes.

The others have disappeared, I don't interrupt him. I listen to him without listening: his ardor, the juvenile side of him, his excesses of tone—all his battles against the philistines in his profession, against the short-sighted administration indifferent to suffering, and particularly the state of neglect of orphaned children—Mahfoud will never grind himself to a standstill: even laid low, his slightly nasal voice remains and pierces the absence.

12

So why do you reappear, back in time, fifteen years before, at those parties filled with such continuous gaiety: my living room, that season, would fill itself up with fifteen, twenty guests—we would decide in the morning; Bahdja who did the cooking would agree to prepare a couscous ("for fifteen or for twenty, what's the difference?"—she would get to it straight away, looking forward with pleasure to the party).

To put an early end to the rehashing of events in Algiers, two or three of us, always the same ones, would insist: "Music, songs, dancing!"

Do you remember, Mahfoud, one evening, two evenings, three evenings: at least! The only man I could dance with, I who claimed, and still claim, only to dance on my own: I don't know how it happened, you became my first partner.

I, intimidated, through friendship not daring to tell you of my reticence: suddenly, because of the rhythm chosen or because, truth be told, of you, I was slipping against you, circling around you, gamboling: the duet was going on forever—for whatever reason, your lightness, the joy in your body, your sureness as a dancer? I used to think I could never dance "their" dances—the waltz, not the tango, no, but the java, but swing, but... You were asking, in the heart of the rhythm even: "What do you mean by 'their'?" I didn't dare reveal to you that I was more primitive than you, more... The dance would carry on endlessly, my head would be swimming, without my feet, still sure, ever stopping, that might last, the whole night long, the faces of the others reeling, the drawing room being too small, we would need an infinitely large stage, we spring forward, we bend, I happily discover that to dance as a couple can become pure pleasure, and not an exhibition, a sense of ease: you wouldn't touch me, the slightest brushing of the arm or the elbow you'd bring back towards you, you seemed so light, so...

Between two dances I finish by sitting down: leaving room for the others, to watch you dance with others. I was trying to catch the eye of your wife, Annette. I press myself on her suddenly. "Now you dance, so that I can watch you together!.... I stole him from you!" and Annette: "I'm not very keen, but it's true, Mahfoud dances so well!"

I slip back into a solitary dance, while around me three or four couples whirl round and round. So grateful afterwards for this discovery, still out of breath, saying to you: "So, two can dance together, with the same intoxication!" I remember shouting out loud in front of everyone, perhaps the second time or the third, since it was understood that we danced well together:—"Oh Mahfoud, you who are said to be the best psychiatrist in town, oh Mahfoud—and going back breathless to that samba—you really are the best dancer in town! I'll swear to it!"

I remind you of that complicity.... From now on I imagine us half entwined gliding through the air, as though in a painting by Chagall, high in the sky of Algiers, above their genuflection, their suspicion, their feverish aura, their overflowing religiosity...

13

During the morning, a few hours later, I am loafing around the campus: the pleasure of being a spectator: midday, today a special "happening" to denounce the present situation in Mexico. A giant marionette looms over the crowd, full of curiosity: "The Mexican president!" The guerrilleros arrive—or rather students acting this romantic role: two or three of them are applauded.

I come across Naima, a physicist from my own country, who has been here for at least two years. I ask her for news from Algiers.

"I got to the kiosque too late to manage to get a French newspaper!"

"They announced nearly a hundred dead at Barberousse: but a truer figure would be at least two hundred!"

"Barberousse?" asks the Arab student, who is trying to calm me down.

I explain the symbolic power of the place to her: a prison, on the heights of Algiers, where in 1956 the French guillotine had its first victims. The present powers that be have just "suppressed a riot": true, three or four guards were killed—and horribly—by the rioters. The following morning "the forces of order" went into the prison, they must have fired indiscriminately: at least two hundred dead— rioters and non-rioters—between four walls! That's the way they think they're fighting the integrist cancer, "whereas," I commented, with tightened throat, "there'll suddenly be two hundred families, two thousand people perhaps, pouring in to join the Islamist faction, the faction of the desperate! How shameful!... And those who carry out this kind of repression claim to embody the law!"

"But Madame, don't be naïve, there does exist an integrist International. I can present you with several cases that I personally have experienced, both here and in Germany!" softly remarks a doctoral student (several of us, all from the same country and feeling homesick, had gotten together for a weekend lunch).

"Doubtless," I reply. "Blood brings blood in its wake. We're rediscovering that logic, but what do you say when those who set themselves up as guardians of the law apply the law of retaliation?"

14

It's with M'Hamed, as it happened, the very next day, that my conversation is the most tense; in the empyrean of the wise, the scholars, the blessed, M'Hamed occupies for me a special place: eyes cast down because of his modesty, and with a half-hidden smile which I alone can see. How pleased he was to find his own true fulfillment: this man whose life was to close in interminable minutes of suffering of the flesh, after he had exalted, oh how often, his belief in justice. M'Hamed, I can see it, radiates, separated from me by an impassable ether; M'Hamed whom I can make out, to whom I imagine myself speaking—an unfailingly gentle presence with a secretly throbbing faith—(*Oh our dearest friend, I don't dare speak to you, the frontier you have crossed is that of martyrdom, I know: the reserve that is so much part of our friendship would find only words of fervor, if in spite of yourself, you were to approach!...*)

That is why, this morning, I seem to be barely mumbling in front of my friend, as I read his response: he is far away, yet he seems so close. The aura of his vision could make our overlapping words shine, but as he grows faint with the early sunlight, I know that within me will remain the words, perfectly clear, sharpened, polished even, of our nocturnal exchange.

I made clear to him my disgust, my shame:

"You well know, M'Hamed, Barberousse, the prison Barberousse, is a symbolic place for all of us and has been so for more than thirty years! The place of the first martyrs, just above the Casbah, heart of the capital, heart of the resistance both audacious and joyous!

"Return, M'Hamed, to the time of our adolescence, both of us students, myself in Paris still, and you from your high plateau, barely landed in Algiers more or less in a state of siege—the bombs bursting, the victims on both sides, children in their arms, falling, and a few young women who had been raped, sexually abused, were proclaiming their revolt in court. You could evoke this bloody lyricism in a few concise words, in your own way, so you understand, the language of your work rises in protest out of its own dryness, and through modesty, but still with a smile in your eyes (in spite of the aura of your image in front of me, I perceive your features, or rather the serenity exhaled by your features), you feel that you have to be quoted... so then you whisper two long lines from a very ancient poet, no, not a mystic you tell me (you understand that with just a hint of irony, I tend to freeze you into an image of piety!), no, a "philosophical bard."

I've forgotten the lines, forgotten the poet—I'll find your quotation, I really must! For the one occasion when you speak to me in a literary style—an obvious effort to move me—me, alas, abandoned by my friends in a single stroke, the scythe cutting both too frequently and too quickly—; before, remember, with your dry discourse, your sociologist's tics overflowing, your sensitivity, I might even say your tenderness towards each and all, muzzled beneath your calmness, your taste for the impersonal!

15

"There are memories which revolt against being divulged without consultation. So they refuse to collaborate, they escape or conceal themselves, as in a game of hide and seek. So, when I speak to you of Zabana..."

It's no longer me, in a half dream, talking to M'Hamed, but, ten years earlier, Ali, a friend, in the room of Kateb Yacine—soon to disappear—trying thirty years later, to bring back to life the days of his youth to Yacine, his closest friend. His days in Barberousse-Serkadji, "silent fortress, closed off from view by a surrounding wall that separates it from the city," he writes.

June 18th, 1956. The young Ali, twenty-two years old, the youngest of those under sentence of death, is, with Ahmed Zabana, the only one to know what is going on: that day, in Paris, Zabana's lawyer is summoned by the president of the French Republic, René Coty, for the appeal for mercy. If he is reprieved, Zabana will live; if not he will be guillotined within twenty-four hours...

That day the so—much—hoped-for telegram announcing Zabana's reprieve never arrives. Zabana, in handcuffs, walks round the prison yard with his young friend Ali (the only one to wait with him, the only one to know) among so many other prisoners. He understands, with impassive face, that he is seeing his last day, that "they" will come in the night, just before dawn, to fetch him for the fatal moment.

In the middle of the afternoon he gives his lesson as usual. Ali, his friend, comes over and notices the sentence that, this time, he takes upon himself to dictate and explain to those less educated than himself: "Study!...

Knowledge is the noblest life and ignorance the worst of deaths!" the other prisoners—some peasants, some older than the master, some...—repeat, take apart, and transcribe the sentence under his surveillance.

"Time passed quickly," recalls Ali under the eyes of Yacine who is listening. We would have liked to live it backwards. The exercise period was over. It was the last time that Zabana would see the blue of the sky!"

Ali then recalls "the shortest night." His friend gives him a present: a Koran and his notebooks. Then he writes a letter to his mother, and is back at prayer, when, in the corridor, night barely having come to an end, the steps of the prison guards arriving in a squad, wake up all the prisoners; the steps stop in front of Ahmed Zabana's cell.

"Ahmed Zabana, the first Algerian to be guillotined, and at Barberousse," murmurs M'Hamed, and then he sighs, seems to withhold a breath. And he adds, I could barely guess at it, the formula of ritual benediction.

"Zabana and Ferradj," I reply. "We always associate the two victims of the guillotine of that night!"

They are dead, the two of them; executed by guillotine at dawn that morning, one after the other: Zabana and Ferradj.

But we have forgotten or, to be more precise, we want to forget that they died differently: the first one in the fixed light of calm heroism. ("I die, my friends, and Algeria will live!" In the corridor, Zabana's voice loudly repeats that last sentence of hope two, three times; the silence of those who, now awake, are listening to him becomes the tombstone honoring this death!)

The second one, Ferradj, oh the second one! The chroniclers of that June night sometimes sigh with an embarrassed smile of sadness: "He didn't know how to die, alas, poor man: he screamed, he shouted, he fought, they dragged him like Aïd's sheep; in the end, he fell silent when they managed to get him out into the main courtyard. What a shame!" they conclude; and sometimes some of them add, dare to add: "He should have died like a 'true' Algerian!"

Ferradj died like a man (why do I find myself talking to my shadows this way, to M'Hamed and also to Mahfoud, who has come back?), Ferradj, whom they wake up in the middle of the night from a deep sleep and who, taking a long moment, eyes wide open, comes to understand that so many guards in a circle around his bed must mean they're going to drag him off to.... He screams, he wails the horror of the nightmare before him: he was one of the last on death row: three, ten others ahead of him presumably went to the guillotine singing, and he, too, would have prepared himself!

Ferradj died like a man who had neither the time to believe in this grim death nor to anticipate it, nor even to imagine it: in the night, to isolate him and have his cellmate sleep elsewhere, they claimed there was work to be done on the toilet on the floor above: he believed it, he slept by himself, he even neglected to say a prayer...

He died like a man, Ferradj, thrown into a tunnel, the victim, designated to be judged, to be sentenced: he wasn't even "guilty," Ferradj, a farmhand on a farm in the Mitidja—one among tens of thousands. The farm of the neighboring colonial settler had burned: resistance workers, of course, who had come in the night. The next day, investigators found an old worn–out bicycle thrown into the bushes nearby: Ferradj's bicycle. He recognizes it when they drag him before "the evidence." Evidence of what? He doesn't get it, poor guy: because of a lost bicycle thrown into the bushes his life ends, his children without any means of support! It goes too fast: Ferradj says nothing more: the investigation is completed, the judgment takes place without delay; he is found guilty without a lawyer. He stammers at the hearing.

He is condemned to death: the settlers of the Mitidja can sleep in peace; in the middle of the summer of 1955, organized resistance near their properties need not be feared: just a few local madmen.

In Barberousse, Ferradj gradually discovers a new world, a community: political activists of all ages, from Aurès or Orania. Ferradj grows accustomed to leading a purposeful life: he takes courses. He learns to read and write.

That night of June 18th, 1956, Ferradj was awakened:

"They want to kill me! I don't want to die! No, no! They want to kill me!"

Then nothing more. They dragged him off.

One last time, Zabana's loud voice (an activist since well before 1954, politicized, who in Barberousse thought only of others, who the year before, surrounded in a cave with other fighters, put a bullet in his right temple so as not to be caught alive. He did not die: the bullet came out through his left eye without touching the brain. They caught him; they treated him; they gave him an artificial eye: then they brought him to trial and condemned him to death in the court of Oran. He appealed to the court of Algiers, which confirmed the sentence. René Coty denied clemency: Zabana learned that a few hours before.... "I die and Algeria, my brothers, will live!")

Twenty years later, the prisoners he taught up until his last day would write on the blackboard of their rural classes before starting their courses—Ali saw this and attests to it: "Study.... Knowledge is the noblest form of life and ignorance the worst of deaths!" Ahmed Zabana.

16

Thereupon Mahfoud's sharp voice, which could be the voice of an adolescent or of a child in the rural class learning Zabana's motto as each day begins, that voice asks me impatiently:

"So why are we talking so much about the Barberousse prison?"

Is it M'Hamed, is it me, bitter, who I hear responding? I don't know who it was retorting gently:

"Yesterday perhaps, or only three days ago, armed men came into Zabana's, into Ferradj's cell, into the corridors of death row, and elsewhere, too, into the cells of those sentenced for their politics: after twenty-four hours of surrounding the fortress, without the country's president having to study a reprieve, without there having been any sentencing or appeal for some of them, armed men behaved as outlaws in the name of the law; they fired into the crowd."

Then Zabana's voice is heard, however weary, sad; it wants to fly off far, far away from Serkadji; it exhales one last time: "I die, my friends, and..."

It grows fainter as the cries of Ferradj return, for he doesn't understand, for they don't understand, the prisoners of yesterday and the day before yesterday: "They're going to kill me, no, no..."

Then the lone voice of M'Hamed chants—from where he is, he sees. He becomes the witness of the massacre that feeds on its own entrails of black blood. From where he is, he can only express compassion:

"You're right," he adds in a tone of infinite weariness. "What did that mean when, in yesterday's usual prose, they made the comment referring to Zabana and his peers: 'They died like true Algerians'? (He hesitates.) True Algerians!.... From now on, let them die as men, as human beings!" he, yesterday's torture victim, concludes. But he is free, he...

This time, because of the scanned rhythm of his lament, it seemed to me that M'Hamed was expressing himself in Arabic where breath and vibration dwell, the ample phrasing of the poetry peculiar to his tribe of nomads and of the recently settled: the Ouled Sidi Cheikh.

17

I no longer know how my American visit continued... One month later, the conversation with my dear departed picks up again, but finely minced, often inaudible, hollowing its bed out in my memory like a wadi losing its rare water and then finding it again... and always, this is true, before the first rays of light penetrate my bedroom.

I laugh. I hear myself laugh, Kader. Suddenly, the performance of Gogol's *Diary of a Madman*, which you adapted in Arabic, comes back to me. My mother, my daughter, and I are in the first row of the municipal theater of Algiers one evening.

You are alone on the stage: from my seat below you seem taller, heavier, to me, but leaping, too, light on your feet as you cross the stage in an instant, then freeze at the edge of darkness.

And your voice, large, metallic, sometimes warmer; and Gogol's words in Arabic:

"Oh! What a tricky creature woman is! Only now do I understand what woman is. Until now, nobody knew with whom she was in love; I am the first to have discovered that. Woman is in love with the devil. Yes, no joke. Physicians write absurdities, she is this, she is that.... She loves nobody but the devil!"

I can't help laughing out loud; an irrepressible laugh I try to contain. I know that you hear these peals of laughter I'm making an effort to hold in, you recognize the sound even though, a moment later, you become motionless, completely inhabited by the character:

"Today, they shaved me even though I shouted with all my might that I didn't want to be a monk. But I can't remember any longer what became of me when they began to pour cold water on my skull. Never before had I endured such hell!... I suppose that, implausible as it seems, I have fallen into the hands of the Inquisition!"

I am silent, I control myself. Every now and then, my mother, wanting to be discreet, touches me with her wrist, meaning: "Don't be such a noisy spectator!" I can't help it: as an actor, but also because of the flavor, the almost rural tinge of your Oran language, your effect on me is almost automatic: I laugh again. I stop. Three sentences later, my laughter takes over again: one or two bursts.... Silent and serious at last, I listen; my very real pleasure in seeing you truly occupy the whole stage, constantly moving, at the same time in St. Petersburg and in Algiers, I give myself over to it as to an inner deliverance: thus you carry all of us, men and women, away with you. Thus you tie up the seams, you reestablish the bridges in this black city (we're talking about Algiers in 1984 or '85), this snarled country that, except for you, is stifling and stinks, but that you set free from so many poisons, in the time it takes to give a stage performance in the people's language, I was going to say very much the people's language. You lighten it with laughter, tears, momentum, gentle irony, and quiet enthusiasm.

Kader, I'm laughing, you hear this laughter surging behind your back; I am not alone, that evening it's a full house, we are joined together by you: you are both Gogol and Kader, you are an actor in the bounty of his art, taming his audience—most of the time stubborn or fossilized, this audience—and at the same time you are gliding above this land through your words, your passion, and your breath.... On that stage, Kader, you embody all of us, that evening when my peals of laughter follow you, pursue you, search for you today!

18

Another day from the past, during my film shoot in Tipasa.

I had the benefit of a crew of fifteen technicians, several cars with two or three drivers: this was the day we paused, when one of the drivers offered to take me to Algiers—I wanted to check the rushes of the previous week in the lab (this was the first color film to be printed in the country).

That same day when you were telling me on the phone that you had to take one of your assistants to the airport, I somewhat quickly suggested I'd come and get you at the end of the afternoon: we would go to the airport together, a production car was available to me. It turned out to be the driver's day off. No matter: I rented a taxi—without a meter—and succeeded in persuading the driver to accept his usual commercial fare.

We joined you, we took the assistant to the airport who was off to Oran; on the way we said a few quick goodbyes in the suburbs.

Instinctively, you had begun to be suspicious of something. Sitting next to the driver, you turned around to me several times, you were questioning me in a curious tone: "This really is the production car?"

Of course, the driver muttered some inaudible words. I reassured you: "We are on official assignment. Why question it?"

We stopped again on the way at some other friends' house, for more greetings. I had the driver wait. I would pay for the ride of three or four hours, my teacher's salary could handle it, but it should not be said that you were suspicious of my cover.... You had counted on me and I had promised.... You continued to have a doubtful look on your face. I saw you look sideways at the surly face of the man at the wheel: it was obvious that you were in doubt, but about what.... I was chatting cheerfully with the young woman from Oran. She made her plane on time.

We went back to the capital, you and I. We were expected for the evening with friends. Having arrived safe and sound, I told you a bit stiffly to go ahead and let our hosts know that we were there, we were so very late—once alone, I paid the driver with everything I had in cash plus a check. You, at the end of the path by the door, remarked again:

"Something's going on and I have no idea what!"

You seemed almost unhappy, certainly bothered.

"You have no idea? So what?" I retorted with a deliberate, winning smile.

Kader, Kader, the only time you ever counted on me, and for such a laughable service, was I not going to live up to it? So many, many times before, and later even more, you were always loyal to me: with your time, your experience, your attentiveness!

"You can go away for as long as you want on this trip!" he insisted a few months later, "I can move in to be there for her!"

And he embraced my little ten-year-old daughter; he added:

"Between Bahdja who'll feed her and take her to school and myself, who'll spend the evening with her—really, you can travel without worrying, as long as you want!"

At the time, it concerned my going to Lebanon. A few days later, I decided not to: the war there had started again. How then could I conceive of settling there for a year with my daughter?

The following month I left for Paris to devote myself to the editing of the music for my film. Do you remember, Kader? When I'd arrive with the last plane on Fridays to spend the weekend with my family, I'd find you there at my house, very late...

"Was she worried?" I would ask, since my daughter had fallen asleep waiting for me.

"Not at all!" you'd reassure me. "I performed my most recent play for her, doing all the parts myself!... She wants to come to Oran and see it staged there before my regular audience!"

I knew—I came to know it by accident—that you were yearning for your oldest daughter, raised in Paris and the same age as mine.

Later, much later, you would bring both girls with you to a beach in the western part of the country, for a whole month's vacation.... Later.

19

It is still dark; the window has opened by itself (I'm coming back to that evening near San Francisco: the last one). The fog has lifted. Your body has vanished. Did I see it, that body of yours, no, I continue to wait for the first fragrance of the day through my eyelashes; your presence was your voice, or mine, for I talked more than you. I saw you back again at the other end of the world and you often answered me in one stream, sometimes you laughed, you coughed, you moved. You were surprised, I know, you wouldn't believe that I retained everything, I remember everything, I'm telling you only a tenth of what I'm holding onto; I want you to come back, I will go to the end of every ocean, through the window open like this in the morning, the ridge of the sea facing me, I will imagine us there, in the city!... Your city, admittedly, but mine as well: in a different way.

I never told you this, but I have long dreamed of Oran...in the eleventh century! I've dreamed of the last Almoravid sovereign, the one who straddled the famous Murdjadjo peak in the middle of the night—which you made us clamber up that first day—I can describe the condemned prince for you: he is as daring as you but almost mad—mad with omnipotence—he must have been as generous, as imaginative as you; he has your stature, seems thinner, and with power has come inconstancy—no, he has none of your jovial nature, your activism—, he is presumptuous.

He is the king, but he is pursued: surrounded for days on end by Abd al–Mu'min, the Almohad who resides on his own mountain across the way (the city between them must be barely a village); suddenly, the stormy night. On the peak, he sees he is alone. Deranged, he rushes forward on his horse: and, from very high up, he falls over the cliff.

He died in Oran, in the middle of the night. Not you. I'm talking to you about the only hero I know from that place, who still dwells within us, even after nine centuries.

But you've left me. And I'm not sleeping. And you left them, over there, last year, on the 11th of March.

20

When I thought I felt your presence on the half-open window sill, should I have told you that I did bear you a grudge when, those last three days, we would go to get news of you at the hospital in Paris where they had brought you the morning after the assault (oh yes, you'll come out of the coma, you'll live!).

I was coming and going those days last spring, and all I was doing was soliloquizing, preparing the reproaches I would utter to you when you'd come back to yourself again, to us that is:

"So they told me that you were warned in Oran on Friday, six days before the fatal blow. They told you that a horde of murderers let loose in the city had your name on top of the list! You knew. You kept quiet. You kept on living, going out at the same time, before the breaking of the fast in that Ramadan month. Not changing the day or the time of your anticipated lecture the following Thursday. You knew. You didn't say anything to your wife, your sisters, your mother. You changed nothing about your life!"

You're still not out of your coma. And I converse with you, I pester you: "So tell me why? Why? Out of what sort of pride? Out of what disgust with this vile and sullied country? To confront them? Not believing that you'd fall in your own city, over some cliff, that city whose secret places you showed me, the subterranean passages, the peaks, the crests, did you believe the city would identify your killers for you? Why? Your pride?... Your fatalism? Your contempt? Were you suddenly tired of living? Your refusal to leave? So tell me: why?"

I wait for you to come out of your coma. I'm not in pain. I feel angry; this time I'm sure I'll say it all to you.... I have your sister—the one who resembles you—on the phone, she has just arrived, she hopes also, she moans with despair and at the same time with reproach, because you didn't watch yourself.... She can't go on but.... I harden myself and inside repeat over and over again to you: "Why?" You will come out of your coma and you will tell us what was inside you these last six, five days. You and your city, what nocturnal encounter? What passageway filled with stench, nightmares, having emerged from what inadmissible past? Since the eleventh century?...

I'm waiting for you to come out of your coma.

On Monday, at dawn, your brother tells me the news on the phone: "He stopped breathing during the night, at four o'clock!"

Why? The slightest liturgical phrase of condolence escapes me. Only this: why? The question continues to be thrust at you.

I wandered around in the lobby, the rooms, the streets, my gaze hard: why? The question is for you; not for fate, not for.... Those five days in Oran, you will tell me about them: what were your thoughts when you were sleeping, when you were awake, when you were laughing with your last child, when you were coming and going. Were you actually waiting for them, your murderers? Tell me, Kader, why?

You're no longer at the window. You'll come back. I understand. If I persist in harassing you about those last days, you'll stay silent. For it is for the life that we evoke, the joys, secrets, complicities, irony, arguments, that you'll come back, that you'll talk to me.

Yes, even the arguments: we only had one and we've never spoken about it—not in life, that is. You know very well that I once held a grudge against you. Childishly or naïvely, I'm not sure, but I did hold a grudge against you. Of that I will not speak at all. You gave me a red carnation: I had decided to leave the evening gathering to which I'd gone with you; an evening in Algiers. I left it while things were in full swing and asked the first person I saw to drive me home.

When I passed, half smiling, in front of you, you gave me a red carnation. I kept it for five days.

21

I'm leaving you or you have left me. All three of you or one after another, I no longer know. The spring in Paris is rainy, the days gray.

You will come back. I'm going to try to forget you. You're gliding; your shadows endure, frayed, but down there in the Algerian sky: while so often the rhythm comes back, the rhythm of murders, of the assassinated targets (victims of a killer emerge from the crowd, a weapon in his fist; of other victims, anonymous, suspect, "terrorists," "assassins," "bandits": the circle of words from before! Others pump up the assessment of the anonymous official breakdown, sometimes loudly proclaimed, but so often rubbed out to leave space for a calm before the storm!), while what begins most of my days in Paris is down there, the fear down there, the danger of death inexorably fed down there,—and I know you, the three of you, my closest ones haunting me, distancing yourselves from me, I know you to be permanently settled above the Bay of Algiers in its coldly unmovable splendor, and at the same time contemplating the whole land of Algeria, its mountains, its desert, its oases, its villages...its stench, too, its ugliness, its swarming worms, its crows come back to the trees. I know you to be above the pine and cedar forests, the ones they're starting to burn with napalm again. Again...

II
Three Days

Three white days. Two in June '93, the third in March '94. Three Alger-ian days.

White with dust. The dust you didn't notice, on any of these three days, but which seeped its way in, unseen and fine, into all those who came together for your departure.

A dust slowly forming, which gradually makes that day grow fainter, further away, a whiteness which insidiously effaces, distances, and makes each hour almost unreal, and the explosion of a word, the gasp of an ill–repressed sob, the bursting spray of chants and litanies from the crowd, all of them excessive on the day itself, from then on paled, worn hollow to the point of evanescence.

So, white days of that dust in which tens of witnesses, friends, those around you, who went with you to the graveside, they the followers, there-after caught up; clothed in it stiffly and awkwardly, unknowingly. Dust of oblivion which cauterizes, weakens, softens, and.... Dust.

Three days white with that dust and that mortal fog.

No. I have to say, no. I, who on those three occasions was absent—far away, almost the foreigner, in any case the wanderer, the one silent in separation, the one who repudiated all lamentation, I say, no.

Not the white of oblivion. Of that oblivion: oblivion of oblivion, even beneath the words of the public eulogies, collective tributes, drama-tized memories. No, because all these words, noisy, declaimed, expected, all this noise embarrasses my three friends; and I am sure, prevents them from coming back, to offer us their light touch, to bring us back to life.

2

I ask nothing: only that they continue to haunt us, that they live within us. But in which language?

Already two and a half centuries ago, a man called Dante, permanently exiled from his city, Florence, was to describe this language "the illustrious common speech." "We call it illustrious because, both illuminating and illuminated, it shines forth," he added in his treatise on "common eloquence."

So it is, when my friends speak to me, if I could catch at least a little of their language "linked with poetry"; Dante compares this language of the absent dear to us, who in order to approach us defy the freezing frontier of our lives behind which we take on weight, Dante compares this language—which is like yours, when you come back to me intangibly—to the "perfumed panther," the mythical animal of medieval bestiaries. He adds, and I quote for all three of you:

"Hearing the call of the panther, the other animals follow it wherever it goes, attracted by so much fragrant softness."

Oh, my friends, not the white of oblivion, please spare me that! Just the "fragrant softness" of your voices, of your murmurings before dawn, I would travel to the end of the earth just to take you with me, and thus to hear you, before each dawn's approach.

Nor the white of the shroud! If they had cremated you they would have scattered your ashes over some Ganges or other, and I would still be waiting for you, your bodies so close and never decomposed, your voices, your murmurs or your mumbling! I would see you between my eyelashes, I would hear you close by, against the half-opened window...

Neither dust nor the mists of distancing, slowly, in an unending slow motion which slips tirelessly away.

3

Those three days stretch ahead. The past distances itself, they say: three dead, or three hundred dead, or three thousand.... No.

The unalterable white of your presence.

No; I say no to all ceremonies: those of farewell, those of pity, those of chagrin which seek their own comforts, those of consolation.

I say no to theater when not improvised: to the theater which, even when flamboyant, is constructed out of rage, or the ready-made theatre of Islamic compunction. No.

Three days of brilliance: with me, close to me, you look on at them as I unfold them.

You smile. You smile at me.

FIRST DAY

I

Fatna, headmistress of a middle school arrives to work five minutes before the doors are opened. In the flat, not far away, in the same quarter on the heights of the town, she has left M'Hamed, her husband, still in bed; her daughter Hasna, who was up late last night (she is preparing her fourth-year exams in medicine), won't wake until later.

Behind Fatna her young brother-in-law—visiting them for a few days—has closed the door.

A luminous summer's day. On the way she breathes in the perfume of the bougainvillea in the municipal park. Hardly arrived in her office, Fatma turns to her assistant. The school yard, as usual, is buzzing with bursts of juvenile voices: gradually the pupils line up in front of their classes.

"So what's the matter"? the young teacher, surprised, asks the headmistress.

Fatma moves her hand to her face, to her cheeks.

"I don't know what's happening to me!" she stammers out, wiping away a first tear.

For a moment she panics, not understanding. She stiffens in front of her colleague, then admits:

"I'm knotted with anxiety—for no reason. I don't know why!"

She turns to her desk; a few hasty gestures to calm herself down.

"Off you go! I'll follow you to the classrooms! It's nothing," she adds in lower key, "Probably fatigue."

Left alone, Fatna lets herself go, crying in silence for several minutes: "Why am I afraid? Why this anxiety...?" she asks herself, forcing herself, slowly, back to rationality.

"My son, my daughter.... The exams will go all right!" she tells herself again.

"M'Hamed, overloaded with work, even more than usual: that important meeting at the Presidency this morning, of the committee of experts whose studies he is directing. He worked late into the night to look over his report. The atmosphere in the whole town is heavy. Our little family life in the flat, God preserve us, holds no dramas! Of course, if M'Hamed were afraid of something, he wouldn't tell me..."

Fatna has thought all this through very quickly: in a few seconds. Hands slightly shaky, she's closed the door of the office: she's gone to join her colleagues for the morning inspection.

2

At this very moment three assassins are closing in on M'Hamed in his room, at the end of the corridor. Responding to their intimidation tactics, a neighbor has gotten the door opened with the help of the young brother-in-law; rushing in like a whirlwind, they hurl themselves down the dark corridor, encircling M'Hamed, standing there in his pajamas outside his room.

Hasna, the young girl, woken in a jerk, finds herself with hands tied and thrown back, seated, on the divan next to the telephone with its wires pulled out. A fourth man, standing at the other end, keeps his eye on her. A young dark-haired man, dressed almost elegantly; he speaks good French:

"Today you and your mother are going to weep for your father!"

"What have you got against my father?" protests the young student, rearing up.

The man sizes her up, gun in hand. His tone is cold, his glance ironic:

"You don't know. But he does!"

When, so long afterwards (for Hasna, tied up, it lasted a century), the four men vanished, when, hearing the long death rattle at the end of the corridor, Hasna, having freed her wrists dashes into the room. ("They tortured him," she keeps saying to herself, almost cold, but alert and sure in her movements), she finds him on the bed, his chest half–open, his whole body emptying, in spurts, of blood. "It's too late!" she says to herself, running for her medical kit. "It's too late, no..." her voice hammers out within her as she comes back, and as her hands, almost beyond her control, make all the regulation checks: listen to the pulse, the...

The long death rattle, growing weaker, has just stopped, these final seconds. The medical student's hands are busy, don't shake, come and go, and, finally, close the pajama top on the ravaged chest. All this time, Hasna's eyes scrutinize, pierce, retain with a neutral precision: "Blood, my father's blood!"

She, the young girl, speaks to him, speaks in the familiar form, in the Arabic of daughter to father, delivers all the words of vision, of torture, of life open and flowing, escaping, still sputtering. "Your father's blood!..." The words are then diluted—when, but when, will they come back, in Arabic, her eyes had pondered in Arabic, a crimson Arabic, the words would rise up again, words of fervor and warmth, those words would rise up again, purple and crimson, warm, in Arabic, one day, years later!...

M'Hamed's young brother comes back to the apartment with the neighbors who've been alerted.

The young girl comes out of the room, dry-faced. Closes the leather medical bag.

"My father is dead!" she says quietly.

"May God hold him in his mercy!" murmurs each of the newly arrived, hurrying towards the bed, towards the body, towards the blood.

3

It's nine-thirty. The chauffeur, who was coming to take M'Hamed to the meeting arranged for ten o'clock, is sent to fetch Fatna from her school.

Told of the arrival of the chauffeur, she jumps up in her office:

"Something dreadful! Something dreadful has happened at home!" a silent alarm goes off.

She puts on her jacket; gets into the car. The chauffeur mumbles:

"I don't know what happened. There are people in the apartment! They ordered me to come and fetch you!"

He adds an invocation to ward off misfortune.

Fatna was to say later that in the few interminable minutes of the journey she prepared herself for the most obvious threat:

"They'll have kidnapped my husband!" she thinks, with hardened heart.

4

The elder son—who has just been to his first classes of the morning at the university as usual—is on his way back home. He whistles on his way.

Vaguely he was to remember a friend in the group he was leaving calling out loud: "They've just announced on the radio that an important personality has been killed!"

The son forgot the news. One more murder, sad! He goes home without hurrying. Having left very early in the morning, he's glad to be getting home earlier: he'll work in peace in his room all afternoon, he promises himself with a light heart.

At the entrance to the building, a crowd. Tense faces suddenly all around.

"My father?..."

His voice fails for the rest of the day.

<u>5</u>

In the presidency of the Republic, the meeting of the committee of experts, for the report on "Algeria, Year 2000" is scheduled for ten o'clock.

All the members, researchers and civil servants, are there, settling themselves around a table. One of them notes that usually (granted, the meetings normally take place at the National Institute of Statistics and Strategy), M'Hamed is the first to arrive.

"Well, today he'll be the last. He must have stayed up late last night. Nit-picking as he is, he must have gone over everything several times!"

Ten o'clock in the morning. The session should be starting: M'Hamed is still not there with his overview.

Ten minutes later the double door opens slowly. In comes the closest adviser to the President of the Republic, the lawyer Haroun. His face is ghastly pale.

"I have come to announce..." he begins in French, his voice barely audible. (And picks up more firmly): "The meeting will not be held.... M'Hamed was assassinated this morning at his house!"

Stupefaction, then commotion. The members of the committee get up.

Some of them, leaving the room a few moments later, believed that it wouldn't be wise to sleep at home that night, and even the following nights.

A few weeks later the report "Algeria, Year 2000" resurfaced in several ministries.

"That's not the real report!" one expert was to say, doubtfully. No, that really is the study organized and supervised by M'Hamed. There's nothing in that piece of sociology that would justify a man's death!"

"We have to look elsewhere! The motive, obviously political, lies elsewhere!..."

6

When Fatna, received at home by her circle of neighbors, learns of the murder of M'Hamed, it's her daughter who gets up in front of her and bars the way to the corridor, to the room.

"Don't go in there, mother!" she says firmly.

She adds, in Arabic, with a catch in her voice:

"Its better for you to remember him alive!"

She takes Fatna by the shoulders and leads her to her sister, who has just arrived. She gets the two women to sit down, among the visitors. From now on, Hasna will be the one to look after everything.

The doctor in her: "The body like that, guts ripped out, chest open, then finished off from behind, with a blow to the back of the neck!..." She might not even be able to recognize his features!.... "Oh face of my father...the face of the purest of Muslims!"

Soon afterwards, she gets a visit from a group made up of a doctor, nurses, and two paramedics in overalls, come to take the victim for an autopsy. She leads them to the room; doesn't go in.

The body, under a white cloth, is discreetly taken away, while the two paramedics remain in order to, as they put it, "clean everything up." Afterwards Hasna shuts the door and keeps the key.

She goes back to the sitting room to see friends, relatives and people representing democratic groups. She looks at her mother, sitting frozen.

For one or two hours, Fatna, elsewhere. *(One hour, two hours during which she has plunged into a long uninterrupted conversation with M'Hamed: it seems he really has left her, and forever! That day at the middle school, together, in El-Bayadh, she was fourteen, or fifteen, or nearly sixteen, she knew in silence, that their hopes, their future, their lives, would be the same... And it seems he's left her!)*

Finally, she gets up: she listens to the organizers of the women's associations who have crowded not only the apartment, but also the street, underneath the windows. There's an improvised sit-in, as for previous assassinations: speeches criss-cross, some launch slogans, some chant a hymn...

Fatna finds the words she needs to thank the militant women and ask just for silence. She wants to live this mourning in search of calm: "It is the will of God!..." That is what M'Hamed would have said. She thanks the friends who are there.

"M'Hamed's brothers will soon be arriving. Let them look for consolation in their own way!"

M'Hamed, she can feel, profiles his invisible silhouette close to her, against her shoulders. He smiles at her sadly: as usual, he trusts her. He must know that she will find the correct form: so that his brothers-in-law, rough and chaste, who come from the high plateaux, won't be shocked, either by the noise or the fever of the capital.

The feminist groups stay outside, near the doorstep. They content themselves with jeering at the celebrities coming to offer their condolences.

7

Fatna speaks on the telephone to her father, who from El–Bayadh still acts as her confidant (she, this man's eldest daughter—such an open man—so proud that Fatna, in that distant South was, at the dawn of independence, the first girl to get her baccalaureate).

She gives way for a short moment: she explains to him:

"I'd like him to be buried in Algiers, here, close to me! So that I can go to see him, so that his children..."

The father, a leather-worker, a true artist, reminds her gently:

"M'Hamed has twenty-three brothers and sisters! He belongs to his mother and to them as well! He belongs to the whole tribe of the Ouled Sidi Cheikh!... He belongs to all of us here: he was the link between El-Bayadh and the people in the capital! Not the two or three ambassadors and a few others who were also brought up here. He alone, because you would come back every summer, because he kept up our ways, and because everyone, when they got to your house, knew that they could count on you..."

He manages to convince Fatna that the funeral should take place in El-Bayadh. The whole town (fifty thousand people) as well as all the people coming from the family oasis of Brezina are waiting to pay homage to him.

In the afternoon M'Hamed's elder brother comes in, grave and impassive. He receives the officials' condolences in silence. He does not utter a word on learning that the following morning a special plane—with his family and others close to him—will take M'Hamed back to his native town.

8

Very early the next morning the deceased's two best friends get out of the plane from Paris, an architect from the Casbah and a physician, born in El-Bayadh and classmate of M'Hamed since primary school. The architect, after carrying the coffin to the plane, gives up on the idea of going to bury his friend "with all these military hangers-on."

"Let's look after his transport ourselves, and by road!" he protests.

People remind him of the heat in this early summer; the whole population of El-Bayadh is waiting impatiently; besides, this new airport—the decision to build it was largely due to the disappeared—has not yet been tried out: that's the reason, they tell him, for all this logistical backup by the army.

"It's thanks to M'Hamed that this airport was finally built and now you're going to have an opening, and to put it bluntly, you're going to open it with his burial."

The friend goes off bitterly, suffering at not having been able to look on the face of the man he had been talking with three days earlier. The physician, a childhood friend, offers support to the children, and gets into the plane with the little group.

On arrival, an enormous crowd is waiting: few have gathered at El-Bayadh itself. Getting out of the plane, passing violently through security—made up of men from Algiers obviously, it's noticed—M'Hamed's mother, veiled in white and straight as a lance, upbraids the friend in a harsh voice.

"So, Abderahmane, you bring him back to me dead! So, you didn't know how to protect him either!"

She repeats these two sentences several times in front of M'Hamed's Parisian friend, who crumples, stiffens and settles himself, looking at all those around him; and throughout the seven days of mourning which he will spend among them all, he remembers.

2

He remembers, ah yes—it was his first year at the French primary school, towards the end of the forties: him, in El-Bayadh, him, son of the master of the Koranic school going to the school of the French—and that tall, gangling, dark boy, a nomad's son, they said he had been boarded out in a working class quarter of the town. He and his cousin would arrive first every morning, both proud of their smart red leather satchels—it is said the father, an important caravaneer, had bought them in Cairo, yes really, as far away as that...

Abderahamane is caught up in all those memories: those of secondary school, their leaving, M'Hamed to Sidi Bel Abbes, and he to Oran. In the background, the silhouette of Fatna, the first girl in this extremely traditional region to earn a diploma, who then managed to wait until she could marry M'Hamed when they had finished their studies. These last years, the two families would spend their holidays together in Tipasa: the adolescent children, the wives, all and everyone, would meet up regularly, with joy.

So Abderahmane was torn to pieces by this verbal blow from M'Hamed's mother ("so you didn't know how to protect him either!") just as he stepped off the plane: for more than thirty years it had been M'Hamed rather who had seemed to protect them all: by his advice, by his austerity, even by an imperceptible hint of humor.

Their discussions only became heated over one point: M'Hamed, a Muslim of unshakable and you might say optimistic conviction, was sure that the present crisis, tied up with the different forms of Islam, would ultimately be overcome "precisely from within Muslim culture and thought." Abderahmane was really not so sure.

10

All the brothers of the deceased are there, the sons of M'Hamed's mother—he being the third or fourth—as well as the younger brothers (of a different mother); the sisters and half-sisters, the young girls above all, are there too: a silent troop, a troop of orphans to boot, since the dead man had played an almost paternal role towards all his younger siblings by following their studies closely, the directions they took in life.

The head of the whole family had died only two years before; it was beside his tomb in the cemetery that they buried his son M'Hamed. There was no official speech (important personages, come all this way, were huddled in a corner, a little to one side)—the family had made it understood that they did not want any public intervention.

Only the prayer for the absent was intoned by an old man of the town, all the men standing up straight around the grave in silence.

The women did not enter the premises of the cemetery; except Fatna who, sitting next to her father in a car—parked in a corner near the tombs—held her daughter Hasna tightly against her.

Outside the little cob wall suddenly appeared a horde of women from the town, friends, but also women unknown, young and old; light veils floating around their heads, who looked on from a distance at the burial. And some couldn't help themselves launching brief outbursts: of anger or pain...

"A man like him, and they killed him."

"And they claim to have killed him in the name of Islam! So that's Islam?"

"No, that is not Islam!"

The following six days and nights of the mourning period were criss-crossed with the same cries of revolt.

During one of these nights, one of M'Hamed's younger brothers, perhaps even the youngest, called upon Abderahmane:

"If only," he let fly, still overwhelmed, "they'd killed him with bullets!"

II

Fatna went back to Algiers the seventh day; taking her turn to watch over her daughter, her two sons. She started work again at the school the very next day.

SECOND DAY

I

One morning, when Mahfoud left his flat in the center of Algiers at the usual time to go to the Hermitage clinic in Birmandreis, Annette, his wife, going into their room shortly afterwards, stopped short with surprise: Mahmoud had placed two or three children's drawings in a conspicuous position on his bedside table—old drawings, almost twenty years old, drawings by their children who were now studying abroad. She went closer, took a long look at the table; on the sheets of construction paper, colored with bright fantasy, Mahfoud had placed (so, had taken off and then placed...) his wedding ring.

"What was he trying to say...or warn against?" Annette asked herself, heartwrung.

Certainly, she thought, since the burial in Azeffoun of the young novelist Tahar Djaout, assassinated (a hundred or so friends had made the journey from Algiers, Mahfoud at the head of the enormous cortege climbing the hill, overlooking the sea, where the grave had been dug), from that day of mourning, Mahfoud had taken to speaking little at home; he seemed even busier than usual.

He had started, with sudden haste, to classify all his works, all his publications: this meticulous clearing of the decks made him stay up even later than usual.

But this wedding ring left on their children's drawings? What was he afraid of for them? For himself?

Annette left in turn to go to work.

<u>2</u>

The next day, or rather the day after the next, was June 15th, 1993. At the same early morning hour, Mahfoud drove off at the wheel of his car.

He arrived at the first entrance to the Hermitage, the great gate open as usual. It was nine–thirty. At the end of the drive, he noticed that the barrier—which should have been raised, the custodian at his post on the side—was down. He gave a sharp toot on the horn, undoubtedly surprised that the custodian didn't appear. (They were to find him an hour later, looking haggard, in the big staircase which faces onto the street at the back.)

Two men that the psychiatrist hadn't seen emerged from the shadows where they had been posted on watch. Since the window on Mahfoud's side was down, the first unknown figure opened that door; then his accomplice joined, and both immediately attacked Mahfoud with knives, in the chest and the abdomen.... One of them must have turned the blade again and again in Mahfoud's slumped body.

The killers ran down the staircase. The car was parked in front of the barrier that was still down. The windshield wiper, that had somehow switched on, had started to grate.

A male nurse, coming by chance from behind, immediately alerted, called, shouted, and began to run. At the same time two doctors, the assistants closest to Mahfoud, came running and found the professor unconscious. The crowd behind; a whole shambles...

One of the young doctors briefly checked the state of Mahfoud, who seemed not to have lost much blood. He lived in hope; helped by his colleague, he moved the wounded man to the other side, then turning off the windshield wiper, drove off like a shot. The Aïn–Naadja hospital, the most modern in the capital, was a quarter of an hour from there.

Half an hour later in the emergency ward, the operation began. It lasted less than an hour: the internal hemorrhage turned out, unfortunately, to be very serious. The wounded man had two cardiac arrests during surgery; with the third, he expired.

At eleven o'clock the news spread fairly quickly, and in some of the big hospitals of the town:

"They hadn't been able to save Professor Boucebsi, victim of a murderous attack."

On the one o'clock radio and television news, his death was the lead headline.

<u>3</u>

After two o'clock, the body was laid out in the morgue of the Aïd-Naadja hospital. A number of personalities came—among them, it was already being said, were a number of professors of medicine (this professional body counted within its ranks, it was well-known, as many enlightened and open-minded men as those who had gradually moved into a staunch Islamism); so some of the victim's colleagues had decided never to go out unarmed.

Many of these visitors, who didn't share the often polemical ardor of Mahfoud against the "new obscurantism" remembered the extent to which, over the past thirty years, he had devoted himself to the improvement of the status of the excluded: mad people, abandoned children, distressed women living alone! How many therapy centers, they deplored as they left, were now going to find themselves without support?

The doctors went their separate ways after leaving the morgue. Last March, Doctor Flici, "the doctor of the Casbah," a true militant of yesterday's war, had been killed in his office, where the doors had been open to all! Now the threat hovered over the hospital services themselves.

A month later, the inquiry established that one of the male nurses closest to Mahfoud—who had recruited him six months earlier, aware of his religious ideology, yet satisfied with his exemplary professional abilities—had been the one to point out the professor as a target for the young assassins.

He described the places, told them about the everyday habits of his boss, and simply arranged, for the sake of prudence, not to be there that day.

<u>4</u>

At five o'clock in the afternoon, Mahfoud was taken back to his apartment, which had become a center for the family and a crowd of friends. Annette had already put everything away in the bedroom— first of all, the drawings of their children and the wedding ring. She slipped everything mechanically into the drawer, but, at the same time, left her sister-in-law to call the children in Paris:

"Better they hear about it from us than from some newspaper!"

Soon there began the wake. Cousins, neighbors, colleagues, assistants and a mass of students; some with their wives; children as well.

Annette looked at all these people, with lackluster eyes. The shadow of a sad smile softened her face.

A group of teachers and journalists from the "Committee of Vigilance for Truth Concerning the Death of Tahar Djaout"—over which Mahoud had presided—sat in the drawing room among other friends.

A woman academic recalled aloud, in a dreamy voice:

"At Tahar's funeral, you remember: Mahfoud, as he left us, turned around and exclaimed—Mahfoud who liked to joke about and against everything: "And now who's next?"

At this evocation, one woman, sitting near them, broke into sobs. Everyone stopped speaking.

Shortly before the curfew one after the other got up and went into the back room where Mahfoud was lying, wrapped in a sheet. He seemed to be asleep, his face hardly paler than usual; some of them asked themselves, Isn't Mahfoud going to get up, and with his usual passion, start making a speech? Was he really no longer to hold forth in his old way?

Then, passing one after the other around the bed, they each left in silence, promising to be back at dawn the next day.

It was announced that the body would be raised quite early, because Mahfoud would be buried in Blida, where he had been born, an hour's drive from the capital.

Annette, ostensibly calm, was worried about what time her two children would arrive.

5

"What can I say," a woman teacher asked later, and a friend of Mahfoud that I'd met in a European capital, "What can I say about the raising of the body the day after?" as she recounted the event.

"The inevitable officials were there: the Minister of Education, the Minister of Health, and some other minister. We, the women from the feminist groups who had always found Mahfoud at our side since '89 turned up, of course, among the first to arrive: after bowing in front of Mahfoud—already locked up in his coffin—and after kissing Annette, we took up our stand in front of the building (they'd stopped all traffic at the next crossroads because of the officials and their bodyguards).

"We felt a bit lost. Mahfoud taken off to Blida, and we couldn't

get there, what were we to do? How could we cope with the void left
by Mahfoud?... Suddenly, without any prior agreement, some of us
just sat down in the street. Others followed us. We finished up fifty
or more—the youngest in jeans, others in tunics, and I think some
even with white scarves on their heads.

"So we sang, cried out, protested. Above all, we sang: a kind of
improvised concert... Not like the old-fashioned weepers!

"I remember that one of us started with the national anthem:
Min djeballina... 'From the peaks of our mountains!'

"Other chants followed in Arabic; the occasional one in Berber
blended with cries in French, slogans for democracy, calls to Mahfoud, words of love...

"The officials coming out were looking at us with uncertainty.
For we were inventing, in rage, a new ritual: Mahfoud after all was
the madman's doctor, and we who had struggled, marched in the
streets on the least public occasion, were becoming, now, a little mad!
Yet we needed, more than ever before, his presence: that he be there,
with his excesses, his joy and his generosity!

"We carried on until the cortege of cars was formed; Annette and
her children, family and close friends, set out behind the coffin for
the return to Blida."

The narrator—since then so far from Algiers—stayed there in
front of me, suddenly silent, her big black eyes fixing firmly that day
in Algiers the year before...

6

The day after the funeral, some of the women assistants from l'Hermitage—nurses, one or two young interns—decided in the morning
to go up to the Blida cemetery, there at the foot of the mountains
which had once more become dangerous.

They said that on arriving at dawn in this country cemetery, they had found beside Mahfoud's new damp grave a young boy of seven or eight: they thought that he had been playing there and got lost far from some neighboring peasant house. The child, barefoot, seemed to have difficulty in moving: a young untreated handicapped child, but with a voice that was almost that of an adult. For some time he had been watching the visiting women's emotional meditation.

Finally, he called on them, with a gentle smile: "You can leave in peace: I am here to watch... to watch over the doctor!"

THIRD DAY

"What is your color?"
"Red, starting to fade!"

ABDELKADER ALLOULA
(interview, July 21,1993)

I

Abdelkader Alloula, dramatist, director and actor, died in Paris just before dawn on Monday, March 14th, 1994. The next day, at the viewing of the body, before he's taken to the airport to be shipped off to Oran, I go into the room where he is lying in the midst of his family with my mother and my daughter: for the last farewell.

His face, eyes closed, features swollen. So he died, a day–and–a–half ago. He was struck down the previous Thursday at the bottom of his staircase on his way to the lecture which had been announced in the newspaper: three bullets were fired, two of them hit him in the head.

When he gets back to his hometown this evening, it will be five days since he had lost consciousness.

The sixth day, tomorrow, he will leave the apartment in the Rue de Mostaganem for the last time. He will navigate the streets above a

75

whole crowd: firstly from his home to the theater (a journey he made almost every day, the one he was about to make when he was struck down). The procession will be led by the women: his two daughters, his wife, his three sisters, and the actresses, and his childhood friends, and.... Only his mother will be missing, because she is ill: it is even feared that she will not be long in following him!

2

For the moment, in Paris, and there in that dark room where he lies recumbent, in the hollow of that still open coffin, from my place in the second row, I see him lying down for the first time; for the first time I see him asleep. His gaze? Inward, already.

My eyes don't leave his features. His face has a color which is no longer his, which is not yet that of earth or sand.

He is there because he is sleeping, and his presence is still there for us to see, and because his big wide eyes, so modest and usually so filled with smiles, will never shine again.

The imam begins the *fatiha* in a chanting voice. He intones the sura in silence: around me are some people, men and women, palms open and joined, perhaps they too are repeating the sacred text in time with the imam.

I, from the second row, half–seeing in a haze, the stiffened face of Malek, the brother of Kader, scanning the face of the recumbent lying there, I wish, oh I wish, that he would just open his eyes. I can't do anything about it: it's my only thought, my only litany. My throat swallows its spasms: look, stay silent, overcome the knots twined in the larynx. The interminable *fatiha*: everyone in acceptance with it, or thanks to it.... What is left for *me?* Before me, for another moment or two, Kader's sleeping face. Image of immobility.

The interminable *fatiha*; the voice of the imam, an incantation.

For a second, my breath gasping in jerks has been following the rhythm of the chant. Which comes to an end.

I turn my head. I'm the first to go out. I wait outside with the crowd of friends.

When the closed coffin had left the room and then been hoisted into a hearse—four bearers including two brothers of the man being carried away, Malek with a stiff upper lip, Kamal sobbing—I realized that Kader was dead.

That he was leaving us emptiness.

3

The town was packed—Oran "the beautiful"—when the next day, a Wednesday, they buried him. "They?" The whole region.

First the women, the young girls, the matrons, the old women—and the children, of course. And the funeral procession?

Oran offered itself a whole day of improvised spectacle, as if, after Kader's thirty years of combat within its bosom, it was just starting to learn the lesson he had been teaching, and finally going to prove this to him, he who had been its master yet who thought of himself merely as one of its children, the best able to seek out, to listen to its murmurings, its secrets!

The ceremony, with its tumultuous waves, begins in front of the Municipal Theatre—the T.R.O. which was the place where the nine plays of the deceased were first put on—and continues in the cemetery, which fills up very quickly; from the edges of the town, children and families and people from the surrounding countryside flock in impatiently.

Today that theater is a mixture of genres, in line with the repertoire of Alloula: heavily rhythmic chants, with a suddenly heartrending humor, with a language that is scattered, composite, splintered, pitching between rabelaisian laughter and the mists of sadness (suddenly I know: Kader's word will traverse the centuries of Algeria precisely because of that vitality!)... One word for all, that day, without understanding, all feel themselves, each one, alone, to be the orphans of Kader.

There was eloquence also (one of the great actors of the country, now undoubtedly the greatest since Kader has died). Present at the cemetery was the very concentrate of tragedy: Zoubida—who posed at my side in the only photo that Kader took of me, fifteen years earlier: me as a Tlemcénian bride, covered in pearls and gold to the waist, and that to please his mother whose daughter-in-law I became by marrying Malek—Zoubida, emaciated, face dark and feverish, wanting to sharpen her sorrow, or perhaps quiet it by trying to free herself from it, revolts, her anger crossed with a despairing scorn:

So where are you, men of Algeria, where do you stand,
Now that Oran has lost its lion, its mast!
Where are you then when the best of Algeria's sons fall?

In tears she continues to improvise on this theme, her verses in the Arabic of Oran swelling into laments—and her body reels, and some of the women hold her up, and she declaims, and...

A cameraman who happened to be there had only to take two steps, beneath her, and before she fell, to catch her this way, for this very evening the whole of Algeria receives, petrified, her diatribes.... Zoubida, age-old friend of Kader, teaching French literature in the university, transformed by despair into a weeper, a tragic singer.... She who in the old days was the one who was always laughing!

There were, of course, the officials: a prime minister who stigmatized Muslim integration, and some other minister, who in recalling his years with Kader at the pre-independence Lycée Lamoricière, showed off his personal feelings.

I who was not there at that ceremony, I think, I'm even sure, that already Kader, unseen, was coming and going above the enormous crowd. Happy as in the theater, where on certain evenings, against all expectations, the audience is much larger than normal. He didn't know that he had so many faithful followers: he is happy, as in an enormous *halqa*, that circle of creation and listening of the people. He is happy, as in pure play!

4

While he floats like that freely in the deserted streets, perhaps he already knows. He knows where the next ones are going to fall: here a university professor, the oldest and the most modest (they'll be waiting for him in Grenoble to give a course), there a *rai* singer (he will have been so pleased, a few months earlier, with his concert in New York: pleased to be known elsewhere!) and then a young journalist, an admirer of Kader, someone in whom he confided (who was to fall while acting as referee in a football training session for young kids from a poor quarter).

Wandering in those fringes of the deserted city (everyone is at the commemoration!), Kader alone occupies the void: all the shopkeepers have brought down their shutters. In full daylight and in spite of the springtime sun, Oran becomes a city of the night, Oran who had never known how to sleep completely, Oran...

Here he is at last, in the place where he wanted to return: where recently he felt best, in the hospital, looking after the children with cancer.

He will see them again, forget himself with them, hoping that they don't yet know, that they'll be waiting for him with hope in their hearts. He'd told them, sitting at the bedside of one or the other, about his last play, a translation of Goldoni, *The Servant of Two Masters.* He had told them also that he was preparing a show—a montage of plays and poems by Kateb Yacine: with four or five actors they will go to put on the show in Marseilles, in Paris, and then, of course, in Oran: but they, the children, will have the premiere: he's promised them.

He looks on them now from the threshold of the three big wards: are they really condemned?

"Condemned? No!" he says to himself—for he was to tell me about this conversation later, from the other end of the earth. Condemned, those who die young? No.

So Kader, about to leave these familiar places, for reasons of modesty, prefers to lend his voice to others—so then I hear him at last, for the first time since they shot him in the head, I hear his voice reciting, with no theatrical effects, in an even voice, the verses of Kateb, with a last look taking in the sleepy children.

> *Thus to die is to live*
> *War and cancer of the blood*
> *Slow or violent, to each his death*
> *And it always is the same*
> *For those who have learned*
> *To read in the shadows*
> *And who, eyes closed*
> *Have not stopped writing*
> *Thus to die is to live.*

5

"Eyes closed," murmured Kader in the wake of Kateb.

The last time I saw Abdelkader Alloula in Paris, on March 15th, 1994, he kept his eyes closed.

III
Death without End

Nothing can stand in the way of glory, solitary and solar,
the virtues of a man or a people reduced, primarily by analysis,
to no more than a hollow vessel...but the shame that remains,
after a life of betrayal, or even a single act of betrayal,
is more certain and less likely to be injurious than glory...

A people that is remembered only by periods of glory or men
of virtue, will always be in doubt about itself, reduced to being
an empty vessel. The crimes of which it is ashamed are what
make its true history, and for a man it is the same.

JEAN GENET (*Letters to Roger Blin on* The Screens)

Between a white death and the other kind of death, the one brought on by the accident of chance, or worse, murder with its pulsing roar of hatred—between these two ways out where lies the difference, for us who remain?

We, witnesses of the instant that breaks the path of a friend, or that gently interrupts its flow, contrary to those who are present at the other kind of ending, reaching the conclusion through exhaustion, of what sorrow or what upheaval must we slowly discharge ourselves? As for me, dear friends, the trio closest to my heart, from that land over the sea, the common homeland, when only the skein of the same languages quivers and renders you once more so present!

Is death unfinished because it is violent, because it comes without warning?... the break, the fall might represent to some extent a double death, for suddenly there comes a dive into the pit.

But I want to speak of the other kind of death, I want to evoke the death which breathes out day after day, with muffled steps hardly heard: death expected, the death we wait for, which straddles days, the death of the long ceremonies around the dying—loved ones search for their words, and when they weep, they do so gently, already with that consolation which beads in the tears still dropping on the cheek.... That kind of death, like a glistening flatfish, slips into the river of our memory. Whereas the death which turns up unexpectedly in strife and disgorged blood erupts and violates our sense of time; it leaves us breathless.

Until the absence—after the funeral ceremony of an expected death, when the departure of someone close to us seems a fitting conclusion, that final separation brings a kind of wise sadness within us to the surface, a sickly sweet resignation.

Finally the dead who leave us after a long period of waiting, even if it is crossed with physical suffering, leave almost smiling at us— they offer us an obscure legacy, not only the few possessions which surround them, and which they bequeath to us, rather and more than anything else, they leave us with a startling message: they remind us with an unspeakable melancholy that it will soon be our turn.

However distracted we may be, the dead who are close to us remind us that one day will be for us the day of passage. To be sure, they tell us this in spite of themselves: it would be a privilege, and even a secret source of richness to imagine ourselves getting ready to die.

We may be only thirty, or at least forty (the stultifying dazzlement of youth will have fallen away): we perceive that we are just half way!

And yet, when a father or a mother disappears, in spite of their sufferings, conscious in the moments of intermittent recovery preceding their departure, they look at us: they are still trying to find a way of directing their gentle reprimand: the reprimand we are not waiting for. They are going to "pass away." Finally, as we shall soon verify, that alone counts, the instant of passing away—eyes open, of course, heart fluttering, oh yes. Only the body still quivers, the body sometimes still tortured by the onslaught of medication—the body quivers in the slow-motion of farewell, before being seized.

No; not a seizure, nor even a collapse. Ashes rather, scattering themselves, a progressive isolation rather; the violence of effacement.

I have spoken so long of the death you might call normal (as if to die, even at the age of eighty, were normal, were life!). That I am tempted to foresee everything: the attacks of sluggishness, of clamminess, the gnawing fear, the progressive strangling of the slightest hope, and then the final speeding up of that white death—death of a child even, death of a lover, death of the body closest to your own body that, eyes bulging, watches slip away something of its own end...

They told me on one of my trips back "home" (in the still recent times when I thought that, whatever happened, I had a "home"), they described the death of a great friend and told the story more or less by hints and suggestions.

He was still waiting for his great love to come: for a long time he had paid little attention to himself because he was the eldest son, conscious of his duties on behalf of a younger sister and brother. He had, above all, to keep watch over his orphan sister: to think only of getting her settled. He lived proud and without doubt chaste; was sentimental and modest: a compatriot born in Syria, returned to Algeria, the land of his fathers, amidst the joy and turmoil of the first years after '62.

I knew him ten years later: a forty-year-old of youthful gait and almost childlike gaze. His sister married and left the country; he himself wound up falling in love; he married a young girl possessed of the discreet, calm beauty of an Englishwoman, she the daughter of an imam. My friend told me (he spoke an Arabic of studied elegance, a carefully mastered English, an uncertain French) of the upsurge of his love, a whole year long, of the discretion of their wedding, the intoxication of their long honeymoon in Andalousia. Never, except on his return from a long stay with the Touareg where he had finally discovered everything he had been waiting for, in beauty and in authenticity, of that too long sublimated country—never before had I seen him so intensely happy.

A few months passed. One day, at the weekend, he came back from the tennis court tanned and hardly tired. He had dinner alone with his young wife, who was beginning to be distressed at not yet being pregnant. They went to bed; certainly they desired each other and made love. I can hardly evoke it, hardly touch on it, for fear of shocking my friend's modesty by my tale.

The wife was first to fall asleep, in the arms of the man she loved.... When she awoke, really just a few hours later, at the approach of dawn, her husband—fifty years old, and looking not quite forty—still had on his face a smile of serenity mingled with a strange distraction: the young woman, suddenly alarmed, had just lit the lamp. She forgot herself for one or two seconds in contemplation of that smile.... Only then did she approach her breath to his, and then she understood: her husband had breathed his last while she was sleeping in his arms.... And that smile which gradually, so slowly, disappeared, like a breeze entering the room and crossing it, that smile disappeared.

She shook the warm body, caressed the torso, the arms—which fell back limply. His face—ah yes, that face which had taken on its seriousness once more—no longer looked at her: he was sleeping in the place where he had already arrived—over there, elsewhere!

She straightened up; she called. The doctor, a neighbor who turned up after a quarter of an hour, later reeled off the verdict: a violent heart attack had taken the sleeping man, put a stop to him.

"A painless death!" the doctor murmured.

Of that she was sure: the smile of serenity—like that of the angel of Reims, in stone—was the proof. Painless, ah yes, but death, really death?

Then the young wife, even though the daughter of an imam, invoked not the slightest liturgical formula, no. She howled. Like a she-wolf, she howled.

As this friend died so suddenly, I didn't take the plane from Paris to Algiers to be with his people—to convince myself that he was gone: emerging from the sheets of love, barely twenty-four hours later swallowed in the white shroud, in the bottom of a grave, opposite the Bay of Algiers towards which he had come for the first time, twenty years before, hurried, silent and solitary. I didn't go. I should have.

Throughout the following year I passed often by the building, in front of his sitting room balcony: he would no longer come and wait for me at the airport, then find the time, a few days later, to take me back. I did not want to go inside his apartment: his widow was no longer there. Relatives undoubtedly would have taken it over.... And turning my head towards the Bay of Algiers (that he contemplates from the depth of his tomb, very close by), I persist in telling myself that he, Malek, is not dead; that he is away: that he is going to come back. That he is going to speak to me ("To you alone," he would say, in his extraordinarily refined Arabic, "to you alone can I say how life, happiness...!"). He will come back. And I, what can I say to him, I cannot conceive of his death in the frozen Algeria of those days, where a cold fever was lurking, where already hatred was seeking its wraps of despair in the darkness...

PROCESSION 1

I

Why do I in turn recount the death of the writer, still young and famous, which occurred unexpectedly that 4th of January 1960, on the road to Villeblevin (Yonne): I'm going to reconstitute that same day as it happened in Algiers, in the afternoon. The news turns, hesitates, twists, around a lady sitting by her window in Belcourt.

January days in Algiers, not far from the *Jardin d'Essai*, the celebrated public gardens: the swifts have left, almost all.... Still just a few in the branches of the plane trees. The sharp, almost white sunlight of a cold winter's afternoon. The woman is waiting by the window.

They have come—two neighbors and a relative. They have started to speak: "Albert..." She heard the name three times. What, Albert...? Her mind is numb. She decided, a while ago, to count the days: since they read her that letter last week: "I'll come back before the summer. I'll bring you here for a holiday!"

Since then she has decided to count the days. Yes, she will go, with Albert. Even over there. What is "a holiday?"

She isn't afraid any more in Belcourt. Another attack, a month ago, but not in her street. She so often feels like sleeping. Peace. Yes, she'll tell Albert, and he'll understand: even in Algiers, even with these attacks, these explosions from time to time. Yes, peace, at last, in Algiers."

In three months, in six months, Albert, her son, will come.

The two neighbors and the other, the relative, are still there. They don't speak.... They look at each other.

She lifts her head towards them, from her chair; she makes as to smile. Her lips are about to murmur "Albert.".... She's almost about to spin out a whole sentence, to say that from now on she'll count the days. Six months, then three months, then tomorrow.... Suddenly she gets up, arms stretched out in front of her. They steady her, gather her up.

"We'll stay by you."

Finally she's understood: their silence, the way in which each of them looks at her, their embarrassment. It's come to her: a black veil suddenly falls over her, dressed in black. It has hit her: Albert won't come, he won't ever come again!

She doesn't fall. She sways. The relative takes her in his arms. At that moment her other son comes in: his face reddened and shattered. He runs towards her, arms outstretched. He needs her.

From that moment on, she doesn't know any more: they've taken her towards the other room, towards her iron bedstead. The relative and the son stay there through the rest of the day. She doesn't know any more. Or rather, yes, she does; peace, in this town, really is here: returned like a swarm of silent bees; stretching out.

Albert's mother is going to count the days, the months. Up to six months; then three months. Peace, infinite white.

Six months later, Albert's mother was to be buried right beside her own mother, dead three years earlier: two ladies, the old and awesome Spanish woman and her gentle, nearly mute daughter...

Albert Camus lies almost opposite them, in Lourmarin, on the other side of the sea.

2

At the beginning of autumn 1961 Frantz Fanon, a West Indian psychiatrist who has recently acquired, that same year, an international reputation with the publication of *The Wretched of the Earth*, returns to Tunis to see the G.P.R.A. He's been the representative of the "Provisional Government of the Algerian Republic" in Ghana and Guinea. That is where he felt the first onset of his illness. His wife, Josie, was to tell me at length about those days of waiting and uncertainty in Tunis. The verdict seems worrying: leukemia has made its presence known. They quickly decide that Fanon should get the best care possible: he agrees to go for treatment to the United States. In New York the Algerian delegation to the United Nations includes among its members some of Fanon's personal friends.

They explain, over the telephone, that they've been able to get him admitted to the Bethesda Hospital, three hours by train from New York: its center for the treatment of leukemia has the highest success rate in the country. American Democrats—friends of the Algerian struggle—will be there watching over him.

Josie, thirty-two years old, and mother of a young boy, hopes to be able to go with him. She doesn't express her desire out loud to Frantz ("It'll be a month, perhaps two at the most," he tells her, undoubtedly to reassure her, to reassure himself as well).

She was to admit to me, years later: "Up to the end, I hoped: they, his friends, those who liked Frantz and admired him, it seemed to me that they would understand: that you couldn't send him such a long way to be treated alone, that if I were looking after him.... Clearly they saw him as a man of iron, indestructible! And he..."

She stiffened, then added, hardly bitter: "I understood his point of view; he thought that all the expenses he was incurring were already quite enough for the Algerian Revolution!"

She remained silent, then: "He died alone, in New York, two months later. Alone!" she repeated harshly.

We spent a summer's month together in a village by the sea, half an hour from Algiers. She would get up early; she would pour out can after can of water to wash the veranda floor. We would stay there, all morning long, contemplating the sea. It was August 1988, we felt good: the rest of the day we would be surrounded by our friends, our children.

Josie would recall the past; then become silent. I would work each night, as I heard the fisherman setting out to sea in their boats.

The first days of October 1988, Algiers reached a fevered pitch; under Josie's balcony in El-Biar, adolescents in revolt were the first to set fire to police cars.

The next day and the following days, this time in the heart of Algiers, the army swarmed the capital, and, confronted with peaceful demonstrations, opened fire: six hundred young people were shot down.

From one end of the rioting town to the other, not being able to meet, we would speak on the phone: I still hear today Josie's enraged voice commenting endlessly on the scenes that she'd observed or that people had told her about.

Once more, O Frantz, the "wretched of the earth!"

3

On March 14th, 1962, the novelist Mouloud Feraoun traces a few lines in his journal of the days of war—he has been keeping it since November 1955:

In Algiers terror reigns. All the same, people go about their business, and those who have to earn their living or simply do their shopping are obliged to go out, and do so without knowing too much whether they will come back or fall in the street. All of us, the courageous and the cowards, have reached that point, so much so that you wonder whether all those terms have any true meaning or whether they aren't just illusions with no truth and no reality. No, you can no longer seperate the courageous from the cowards. Unless, through having to live in fear, we've all become insensitive and unconscious. To be sure, I don't want to die, and I absolutely don't want my children to die, but I don't take any particular precautions.

During his last stay in Paris, a month earlier (friends have insisted that he come to Paris "for self-preservation," as one of them put it); Feraoun, who has received several threatening letters from the O.A.S., would smile and repeat that his place was "at home, whatever happened."

He's promised, however, to send his journal soon. Now that negotiations are being discussed so seriously, this chronicle will undoubtedly come to an end on its own! "If only peace could come!" he murmurs, there in his publisher's office.

That day of March 14th in Evian, it seems that the two delegations—those of France and of the F.L.N.—are about to come to a conclusion; will tomorrow see the announcement of the ceasefire?

Algiers, for months—and particularly these last weeks—seems to be completely delivered up to O.A.S. violence. As soon as the declaration of peace is announced, there is bound to be a murderous explosion.

At home, that evening, Mouloud hangs around in the kitchen for a long time: he chats with his wife and his eldest son. He takes his son into the sitting room: starting to recall, in detail, all the schools in which he worked as a teacher. The young Ali will remember this afterwards; he will write to his father's friend, Emmanuel Roblès about it. As it happens they are talking on the radio about Roblès's last novel; father and son listen to the program together before going to bed.

The next morning at eight o'clock sharp, while Mouloud is getting ready to go out—an important meeting at the community center in Ben-Aknoun—his wife wants to wake his two sons: it's time for school. Mouloud intervenes.

From his bed, Ali hears his father remark softly:

"Let the children sleep!"

Then after a silence, he goes on:

"Every morning, you make three men go out! You surely don't think that they'll give them back to you just like that every day!"

His wife, to fool fate, spits violently into the fire. On his way out Feraoun locks the door as a precaution.

By that time already, in the town, the O.A.S. killers are at work; they have begun to reap their daily ration with impunity.

At half–past six in Hussein-Dey, in front of a cluster of Arabs, workmen and laborers waiting for the bus to go to work, a man armed with a machine gun gets out of a parked white Renault car. He empties a first magazine on the crowd, then a second: the count is six dead on the spot, and thirteen wounded, some of whom will die before reaching the hospital.

The meeting at the community center in Ben-Aknoun, where Mouloud Feraoun is headed, is arranged for ten–thirty, and it's Marchand, the director, who is to preside—and who has been living all these weeks as a hunted man. He's received more than one threatening letter, first of all in Bône where, by a miracle he managed narrowly to escape an attack. Posted in Algiers, he rediscovers fear once more: he changes addresses as often as possible, and has given up any kind of family life—he is a "Frenchman from France," veteran of the resistance, veteran escapee from the camps, once having been to Algeria, he asked to come back, in spite of all the dangers: the institution founded by the famous ethnologist Germaine Tillon for the education of children in an "integrated milieu" is a source of exaltation for him.

Some of the inspectors, from the East and from Tlemcen, have not been able to get there; the meeting is put off for half an hour. Mouloud Feraoun, and his two friends, Salah Ould Aoudia, a Kabyle who converted to Christianity, and Ali Hammoutène, a Muslim, are all three on time.

They are there, seventeen teacher-inspectors, getting settled in the room kept for meetings, a kind of hut in the corner of the courtyard. Marchand is going to open the session.

To the side, in the same cluster of buildings surrounded by trees and a large green space, ten or so people are working in the administrative offices; the *École Normale Primaire* for girls is located in the immediate vicinity.

The complex, at a crossroads in the heights of Algiers, is called "Château-Royal" or "Château Douïeb" named after the former owners of the property.

On the road lined with palm trees which runs alongside the buildings, two cars, carrying eight armed men, drive slowly, then park in front of the gateway.

A first man gets out. It is the Arab concierge, sitting by the window at the corner of the *École Normale*, who sees him, distractedly at first. The man makes his way towards the administrative buildings near the entrance.

A little later an employee who was lingering in the courtyard is immobilized in the corridor as he is going back inside. Threatened by a firearm pressed into his back, he joins his other colleagues, all parked in an office: he's had time to notice, in a flash, that all the telephone wires at the switchboard near the entrance have been ripped out.

At the other end of the courtyard, suspecting nothing, Marchand and his colleagues are getting under way with the opening discussions: they are aware of the importance of this meeting, and that it will be very difficult for them to organize the next one, given the threats weighing on them.

It's a quarter past eleven: two armed and agitated men burst noisily into the room, a third man following them, a young man with blond hair, unarmed and looking astonishingly placid.

The first armed man gives orders to those present:

"Stand up all of you, hands in the air, and move back against the wall!"

They obey. Upon which the blond young man intervenes calmly:

"He will not harm any of you. Those whose names are called will have to go outside with us: a mere formality!.... Registration."

Some of the teachers are reassured: last week there were several pirate broadcasts by the O.A.S. Is it an operation of this kind?

Only Marchand remains hardened—and close to him, as a witness was to affirm later, Mouloud Feraoun looks very pale.

The second man takes a list out of his pocket. He spells out seven names one after the other, in alphabetical order. The blond young man intervenes, still just as calm: "Those whose names have been called are to take out their identity cards and present them to us!"

These few details seem to reduce the tension. Besides, one of the armed men is already on guard in the courtyard, the other, submachine gun on one arm, stretches out his other to take the identity cards.

"Aimard, Basset, Feraoun, Hammoutène, Marchand, Ould Aoudia."

The last named, hesitating, asks if he can go and fetch his glasses which are on the table: one of the men gives him an affirmative nod. Feraoun's friend retrieves his glasses, arranges them in his pocket, hands over his identity card, then moves over to stand by the door. A seventh name has just been called three times: "Petitbon!"

Petitbon isn't there. The others, those who haven't been called, have not moved: against the wall, arms in the air, stiff-faced they suddenly look like automatons emptied of all reality. The six whose names have been called then go out into the courtyard in single file, arms still raised, where the two armed men take positions behind them.

The blond young man, in a suddenly aggressive tone, threatens those who remain:

"Above all no one is to leave without my authorization!"

Leaving the room, he closes the door.

A few minutes go by, interminably. When the burst of gunfire breaks out with a heavy sputtering noise, a staccato of what seems to be infinitely amplified, some of those who are there rush to the windows; others were to admit that they were expecting to be led off in their turn for execution. Then comes the strange emptiness after the massacre: a chalken silence encircles them. They look at each other; some at last go out into the courtyard.

At the end, against the corner wall, lie three hunched up, almost

shriveled bodies. The first witnesses to come running—one or two pan-
icking teachers, others emerging, stupefied, out of the neighboring
offices—discover against the other side of the wall, not far from the half-
open gateway, three other bodies: Mouloud Feraoun, fallen on top of his
friend Ould Aoudia, half covering him, right beside Hammoutène, who
seems to be still quivering. The writer is in his death throws.

At that moment the two machine guns which had been set up before-
hand near the entrance (the concierge of the *École Normale* saw everything, powerless), were taken away by the executioners, who calmly
joined their accomplices in the avenue of palm trees; the two cars
started up again, taking away the commandos.

The noise of the machine gun salvo was so intense and loud that
once the frozen moment of stupefaction had passed people came running from all around: they thought for a moment that there had been
a full-scale plastic bomb attack on the premises.

A fifteen-year-old—Hammoutène's son—was playing not far
away: he thinks of his father and rushes onto the road. At a crossroads, he passes the two cars with the armed men, driving away
unhurriedly in the opposite direction. He makes it to the "Château-
Royal." He is among the first to kneel beside the bodies: underneath
Feraoun, still in the throws of the death rattle, they find Ould
Aoudia, with two bullets in his forehead—the last two, that finished
him off. The young boy suddenly recognizes the third victim alongside them. "My father!" he cries out before fainting.

Mouloud Feraoun is the last to give up his soul. On the other hand
Inspector Marchand died instantaneously. He was facing the second
machine gun which afterwards finished off the other two French
teachers.

When at last the police and the firemen arrive, the phases of the execution are reconstituted according to the testimony of the concierge, who expresses herself in her dialect of the Algerian South: apart from the men kneeling behind the two machine guns, two killers fired from each side with their submachine guns. In the courtyard, six armed men in all, methodically went down the line comprised of Marchand and his colleagues, and the other line, in front near the entrance, of Feraoun and his two friends.

"Methodically?" Indeed, the gunmen first shot the expiatory victims in the legs, in cold blood; when they slumped to the ground they took their time shooting them in the thighs. Then, only afterwards, in the chest.

The long protracted burst of fire had suddenly stopped; afterwards a few isolated shots were heard: these were the *coups de grâce* in the forehead of Ould Aoudia, protected for a moment by the body of Feraoun who had fallen on top of him.

In all, one hundred–and–nine 9 mm. cartridge cases would be picked up by the police: the inquiry established afterwards that at least eighteen bullets were fired for each body.

Salah Ould Aoudia's son, alerted to a "serious incident," runs to the indicated hospital: he's the only one allowed to go as far as the mortuary, since he is a medical student. Jean-Philippe Ould Aoudia, who was afterwards to devote thirty years completing minute investigations which would finally identify the assassins (to no avail since they were to benefit from the amnesty granted by the French State for all acts of war in Algeria), would himself describe the instant in which he found himself face to face with his father's corpse.

"One of the attendants said to me: 'Quite right, they've brought us six unidentified bodies, and we don't know where to put them!'

"My eyes have gotten used to the darkness of the place, and I can make out six bodies lined up, lying on the recently scrubbed floor, squeezed together, wearing dark suits, among which I recognize my father, then Feraoun.

"The man is disappointed by this identification of only two of the bodies. He asks me: 'Which flag do we put them under?'

"Since I don't understand the meaning of his question, he explains that you have to cover the coffins either with the blue, white and red of France or with the green and white flag of Algeria so that you can lay out the bodies either on the side of the French or on the side of the Arabs, to avoid arguments."

While the young Ould Aoudia can't tear himself away from the sight of his father's face which, with its two wounds in the forehead, still retains its mask of suffering, he hears someone behind him at last make a reply to the attendant worried about the flags:

"Doctor," he remarks emphatically, "The bullets that killed them bear the tricolor, no?"

At the end of the same day it's the turn of Mouloud Feraoun's son to go and identify his father. He was later to write to Emmanuel Roblès:

"I saw him in the morgue. Twelve bullets, none in the face. He was good-looking, my father, but all frozen, and he didn't want to look at anyone, there were fifty or so, a hundred like him, on tables, on benches, on the floor, everywhere. They'd laid my father in the middle, on a table."

4

In April 1962, the Berber poet Jean Amrouche dies. Born at the beginning of the century in Ighil-Ali (Great Kabylia), he breathes his last in Paris, in the arms of his sister.

All those close to him, his French wife, his young children, form a circle around his bed, but it is his sister who is holding him in the final throes of death—he can only just perceive the daylight through his flickering eyelashes, but he can hear, Taos knows, he can hear them: so Taos sings, with her full voice. She sings in Berber.

Jean's old mother, eighty years old, is getting weaker—she lives in Brittany. No one has warned her of the condition of her favorite son.

Taos is there, present on behalf of the tribe back there in the place where neither Jean nor his mother will return.

Life in the village: while Taos is singing of joy, Jean is looking through his half-closed eyelids; he sees an approaching vision of a permanent spring, that of his childhood, of his constant return visits, of his breathless dreams. The most recent trip—this last year he has been continually acting as messenger between De Gaulle whom he admires, to whom he represents his own people, and over there "the commanders" that he meets in Switzerland or, lately, in Morocco: the peaceful Ferhat Abbas, the pharmacist, and the other one, the warrior—a peasant born out of the same mountains who looks Jean, the Christian Kabyle, up and down with his quizzical gaze—the prestigious Belkacem Krim.

In the eyes of these men of his own blood, of his first language, Jean becomes the herald of the other, of the old French heroes (suddenly the old dispute flaps its faded wings: his father offering resistance, in Ighil-Ali, when the grandfather would say *à propos* of Jean and of his two other brothers: "He's five, the kid. Tomorrow I'm having him circumcised!" and his father, usually so docile, would stiffen and find the strength to oppose him: "My sons are Christians, like me!" Yes, a scene like that, in Ighil-Ali in 1910, or a little earlier! Afterwards, the emigration to Tunisia. The family squabble seems never to have been resolved).

Now Krim Belkacem is scrutinizing Jean, he turns towards Abbas, then decides to confirm the message for the French chief: twice, three times in the space of a few months, Jean Amrouche, poet, publisher and man of letters, has become the messenger! He has started to dream; likewise his friends: tomorrow in the independent Algeria, he would be in charge of Culture (an Algerian Malraux in a sense!).

April 16th, 1962: it's the last day of the poet Jean el Mouhoub, who has drawn from the living springs of his aged mother's Berber songs. "The white voice of my mother," as he had written magnificently.

Fadhma Aït Mansour is waiting in Brittany; she had begun herself to write some time before: past the age of sixty, in French. She was to dedicate her story to Jean, for she thought to be gone before him.

This morning it is Taos who sings of the tribe, of all the singers and poets of Ighil-Ali, of all the thorns of emigration, of all the pains and fears of the war that is about to come to an end. Jean becomes the link between "those" back home and De Gaulle; Jean is the olive branch announcing the first breath of air. Jean is breathing in the arms of his sister.

Taos, the warrior, draws herself up; she bays. The flesh of the language, the buoyant curve of the rough, indelible words, rasping time like a harrow under the oak trees, the words rise up, and at the highest point of their flight, carry away the poet who can no longer make out the rays of the Paris morning sunlight. Who, at the very last moment, can hear the murmuring of the Kabyle village under the snow, the village where he was born fifty-five years ago.

So then, Algeria reveals herself on the first day of independence (I was there, I arrived early, by the first plane, a smile on my lips, with eager eyes, and I walked, tirelessly until nightfall that day, my twenty-sixth birthday, and the next day), so then Algeria presents herself, stripped recently of these four writers—above all, it's true enough, orphaned of nearly a million of her own (the resisters, the victims, the anonymous mass of bodies hidden in the woods and in communal graves: women, old men, children, the innocent ones, sometimes left stupefied, their eyes always open).

As for these four men of the pen, who disappeared during the last two years of the war—they were each only just beginning to taste of their own maturity! They were each in his own way waiting for this dawn—even Camus who did in fact in Stockholm let out a sigh for his mother, Camus, had he been there in 1962, would he have resigned himself to come and get his mother and take her away in the midst of the exodus of the "poor whites?" No doubt; he would have died afterwards, much later.

Camus, an old man: it seems almost as unimaginable as the metaphor of Algeria herself, as a wise adult, calm at last, at last turned toward life, ordinary life.... In the same way, is it possible to think of Algeria as peace-loving, with her dignity restored?

And why not as a peace-loving man? Why always Algeria "my mother," my sister, my mistress, my concubine, my slave? Why in the feminine? No.

Four writers never saw, in those early days of July 1962, either the explosion of joy, or the frenzied ecstasy which danced so lightly, at last free of care.... But, July was not yet over before, not far from Algiers, the so-called "national" and "people's" army was firing on Algerian resistance fighters—the *maquisards.* Less than a month after the vote for independence (the premonition of the Algiers crowd on the first days, and that cry rising up from the Casbah, reaching up to the heights of El-Biar with its protest: "Seven years, that's enough!").

Mourning here lasts forty days. The festivities were over in less than thirty days.

"Seven years, that's enough?"

But no: the blood returns, flows fresh and black, because it's between supposedly fraternal combatants! On the decks of the last boats pulling away crammed with *pieds-noirs*, those who have kept their hunter's eye can see up on the slopes of the Atlas forewarning of the divisions to come!

True, it had all been in the offing before '62: had Frantz Fanon already glimpsed that fracture that comes before the final break in '61 when, worn out, he resigned to seek treatment, strange irony, not far from the land of his birth? Did he already suspect the coming of the time of the jackals?

As for Jean Amrouche, when clouds first darkened the sky, he would no longer have wanted to leave Paris for Algiers or Ighil-Ali, and Camus, well Camus the Algerian would have finished his novel, *The First Man*. And other mysteries, for him as for us, would be less so...

These four dead hopeful ones, I imagine them pen in hand, watchful during that summer of '62, over the long procession of dead fighters: on the road, they too march in line, to inaugurate this new beginning.

The tribute in warm bodies to the new Algeria, panting, tortured. Would it begin to gleam in that sunlight: the *chahids* or *chouhadas*, as they were known, that is, literally, "the martyrs in God's name?" Why not the *abtals*, the war heroes, the volunteers who offered their lives, their ardor, why already that hyperbole, and by suspicious consensus? We missed Fanon, who would have made a protest in the name of semantics: he more than anyone else ready to pull out the scalpel of his lucidity.

And Feraoun was writing several months before his death: "Soon, we can feel it, the end will come. But which end? The most banal, perhaps, which will also be for each of us the most logical. Perhaps also the most unexpected, which, after the fact, will appear to be the only one possible, the one which each of us will swear to have thought of, which will astonish no one yet will anger each of us, and which will finally allow those who are still there to start living again, to begin by forgetting."

These four heralds—I was about to say the abtals *of Algerian literature, an unfinished literature—I call them to me today, I raise them, my exemplary brother-writers, on the edge of the quagmire: let us look deep into it, let us together question other absent ones, so many disturbing shadows!*

Together, too bad if it is thirty years late, let us at least bring back the strangled, the suicides, the murdered, nestled in their somber history, in the hollow of tragedy.

THE SPECTER OF POST INDEPENDENCE

I

Edouard Glissant told me recently about his last meeting with his compatriot (and mine) the Algerian-Martinican Frantz Fanon, whom he saw briefly in Rome, undoubtedly around 1960, shortly before Fanon's illness.

"He told me over the phone to meet him at a certain address that very evening: I found the place; it was a brothel!"

The two men sat chatting in the *salon*, admiring the ladies of the establishment, then, once outside, quickly went their separate ways: Glissant understood that even in Rome, Fanon put his anonymity above everything else, for reasons of personal safety. Before disappearing into the night, face watchful, eyes looking about inquisitively, he made sure that he wasn't being followed.

So, Fanon died, not far from New York on December 6th, 1961. I reported on the funeral to Glissant: Colonel Boumediene, the lieutenants closest to him, all those who for the past two or three years had adopted Fanon as their political and philosophical master (whereas, if Fanon had come back to life ten years later, he would have turned his back on these new masters, he would have gone back and shut himself up in his hospital in Blida), so all these men, more the Bonapartists of a military state in the making than the "revolutionaries" they liked to proclaim themselves to be, had at least on that occasion, a theatrical sense worthy of a secular and progressive Algeria.

They bore the psychiatrist's body onto Algerian soil—two or three kilometers beyond the Tunisian border, before you see the electrified barbed wire and fortifications of the Morice line on the horizon. The trumpet sounded the Algerian national anthem; the forty-odd officers and non-commissioned officers saluted the raising of the flag, then the burial began in silence.

Among them, a young woman, eyes hidden by dark glasses-my friend Josie, who told me of the ceremony later—froze, looking towards the horizon—there in the distance was the little town at the foot of the Algerian Tell where she had begun her married life twelve years earlier.

Henceforth Frantz was there asleep, at the eastern tip of the country which he had adopted from the outset.

The middle of that year of 1962 was to know the effervescence of independence; already the open splits between the leaders were reappearing on the public stage. As we left those seven years of childbirth behind, what could we then illuminate but ghosts that no one wanted to evoke? It was as much as we could do in that autumn of '62 to whisper, at least for some of us, the travesty of their end.

2

Under the impetus of these four writers, who died on the eve of independence, here I am, going back in their company over two years on which the war hinged: 1956 and 1957.

In '56, after a year–and–a–half of conflict, many people hope for, and even glimpse, a possible way out: a halt to the murderous brutality of both sides, and that thanks to a truce, through dialogue and official contacts sketching out a possible peaceful solution: an independence in stages where the various communities might live. Utopia? It is so easy to judge it that way after the fact.

The war is at the end of its first breath: solutions are glimpsed which might muzzle it, but it will quite soon be too late. The mortal hydra will regain possession of the whole terrain: four, five, or nearly six years will go on vomiting out their dead and the wind of their violent actions.

The year 1956 really opens in January with Albert Camus's lecture at the *Cercle du progrès*.

In the *Place du gouvernement* just around the corner, thousands of European extremists—the *ultras*—shout slogans: "Mendès France au poteau!" ["Mendès France to the gallows"] and "Camus au poteau!" ["Camus to the gallows"]. Inside the hall (some of the windows soon shattered by volleys of stones from outside), Albert Camus, pale and tense, but determined, reads the text of a speech calling for a truce. On the platform, Ferhat Abbas, the moderate Nationalist leader (who will only join the F.L.N. a few months later) listens to the writer. Nationalist Muslims and liberal Frenchmen mingle and fraternize. Later on, this scene would seem to belong to another epoch. And yet, this dialogue might have led to an Algeria which, like its neighbors, claimed independence without too bloody a price. All Franco-Algerian links would not have been smashed in a single blow: a solution like the one Mandela found in South Africa could have been reached.

But instead the law of arms prevailed (hundreds of thousands of French soldiers, including reservists, on one side; and on the other, a few thousand *maquisards* in the *djebels*, a few hundred "terrorists" in the towns). Holding sway over heaps of civilian dead. Nineteen-sixty-two was to see the constitution of an independent and sovereign state, but one which had been bled white.

Thus the last public utterances of Albert Camus, who had placed himself at the very center of the struggle: "My appeal is more than pressing. If I had the power to give a voice to the solitude and anxiety which lies within each one of us, it would be with that voice that I address myself to you. I have loved with passion this land where I was born. I have drawn from it everything that I am, and I have never withheld my friendship from any of its people, whatever race. Although I have known and shared the misery and poverty that are plentiful here, this land has remained for me one of happiness and creation. And I cannot resign myself to seeing it become the land of unhappiness and hatred."

This was January 22nd, 1956, in Algiers. On February 6th, the new president of the French Council, the socialist Guy Mollet, arrives in turn. He doesn't dare face the outburst of rage on the part of the European *ultra* demonstrators and, appointing Lacoste governor general of the colony, gives him as policy guideline: "One priority: win the war!" The French recruits are two hundred thousand in number; Guy Mollet intends to bring them up to five hundred thousand.

Operations follow sweeps, sweeps follow dragnets. The *fellagha* resist, sometimes attack; take advantage of the desertions of the native infantry weary of killing their own. In May the annihilation of a whole reserve unit in the gorges of Palestro has enormous repercussions. The *ultras* ask that the prisoners condemned to death be executed.

June 19th, 1956: for the first time in the course of this war the guillotine comes into use. Zabana and Ferradj have their heads cut off in the name of French law. Prisoner of war status will not be granted to the Nationalists.

Djamila Briki, who was in the early days of July 1962, my first friend from the Casbah, recounts her memories—which were fortunately to be recorded, with those of a number of other Algerian women, by

Djamila Minne-Amrane—of the new funeral rites at the gates of the Barberousse prison:

"The families of the condemned men would go to Barberousse every morning, where executions would be posted on the gate. We'd go every morning to see if there were any white notices on the gate; sometimes there were three or four of them, each execution had its own personal notice. We were never warned in advance, you had to go and read the names on the door. That was the most awful thing. And the water!... When there was lots of water in front of the gate it was because they'd cleaned up the blood by squirting it with great jets of water from a hose."

A little later, a guard would appear and call out the family name of the man who had been guillotined at dawn: he'd hand over the dead man's personal effects to his wife or his mother. The women wouldn't cry; their companions, come for news, would gather round them and then go home with them for the religious wake.

The executed man's body was never given to his family; the prison authorities themselves dealt with the burial in the El-Alia cemetery. They just gave the number of the grave to the women, who would go there the next day.

Djamila Briki still remembers one scene in front of Barberousse on a morning when there had been an execution (she herself, whose husband, Yahia, had been condemned to death, would live that waiting and that tension):

"I can still see an old woman when they gave her back her son's bundle (one of those guillotined at dawn). She sat down on the ground in front of the prison gate and took out her son's linen; she was kissing his shirt, his comb, his mirror, all the things that were his. There were never any tears, cries or lamentations. We would leave with the family of the man who'd been executed."

From June 20th, 1956, onward, at every capital execution the watchword of the resistance in Algiers is to increase attacks against all Europeans—with the provisional recommendation that women and children be spared. Yassef Saadi's networks move into action.

The *ultras*, backed up by a special branch of the Algiers police, counter with the terrible attack on the Rue de Thebes: on the night of August 9th to 10th; in the Casbah four blocks of buildings crumble to the ground in complete darkness on top of a hundred or so victims. The fatal mechanism has been set in motion.

These are the circumstances in which the Soummam Congress takes place, shortly afterwards, from August 20th to September 10th, in the very heart of Kabylia—a Kabylia nevertheless staked out by the French army. For twenty-one days, the principal leaders of the *maquis* and the urban resistance will meet to debate their various point of view, and finally define a platform for the continuation of their combat.

This first conclave in which the Nationalist struggle, up to now zigzagging between concerted action and empirical, localized manifestations, seeks a strategy, is in fact the work of a new man, Abane Ramdane (who in '54 was not one of the nine historical founders of the F.L.N., having been in prison since 1950: he was to be liberated only at the beginning of 1955). He has been lying low for at least a year, controlling and coordinating most of the action within the towns. His friend Sadek Dehiles, who was in command of *District IV*, remembers him saying at that time: "You can kill a whole division in the *djebels*: what counts is Algiers!"

It is actually in Algiers, in 1956 and 1957, that Abane works effectively to bring together the different component elements of the resistance—which until then were fragmented, in opposition to each other, or unaware of each other: the ex-Centralists of the old P.P.A. (Party of the Algerian People), the Communists accepting integration into the organization, the Oulémas circuit (Nationalist renovators for a modern Islam, criticizing the *marabouts* for excessive collusion with the colonial administration). Abane doesn't forget the trade union movement: his energy is overwhelming; he gets along well with Larbi Ben M'Hidi who, in June '56 left the district of the Oran region in order to help with the awakening of the capital in Algiers.

At the Soummam Congress, the primacy of the interior over the outside political leadership was proposed. Ben Bella waited in vain in Cairo to go back and take part in the discussions.

It's in October '56 when Ben Bella takes Sultan Mohammed V's plane with Aït Ahmed, just back from a tour of Latin America, as well as Boudiaf and Khider, to go and meet his colleagues in Tunis and make known his reactions to the decisions made at the Congress; at this point, the famous inspection of the plane by the French army takes place: it's the first airplane hi-jacking organized, or at least, recognized by any State.

In the Paris prison where they were to be kept until the end of the war, Ben Bella and his friends were to have plenty of time to measure the loss of their influence.... And five leaders, confined in the same prison for almost six years, were to come out split into at least three opposing clans!

No matter, the movement of history sweeps on: from October '56 to April '57 the uncontested leader of the Algerian resistance is unquestionably Abane Ramdane—who at the Soummam, backed up by Ben M'Hidi, and briefly by the *maquis* leaders Zirout Youssef and Krim Belkacem, criticized the brutal methods and violence among Algerians that Krim's lieutenants—particularly the formidable Amirouche—practiced too readily. It is Abane who will conceive and finalize the eight-day general strike of January '57: when the Algerian question will appear on the agenda of the United Nations, when the world will see that the Algeria of the cities, as well as the townships and the villages is united in the struggle for independence.

To this challenge, that of the "Battle of Algiers," the French government will respond by landing Massu's parachutists, barely a few months after the Suez operation in which they took part. They will commit daily acts of violence and torture, carry out a regular pruning of the population of Algiers.

The balance sheet? Thousands of dead, thousands tortured, a town more or less muzzled at last: some of Abane's rivals were to reproach him for the high cost of this strategy, but later.

Why this digression into the killing fields of '56 and '57? Why, to flee the years '93 and '94, an Algeria cracking with the hollow sound of fracture? Because today, it might once more be possible to hold one's breath, restrain a moment the hammering subterranean step of reaping death, death reaping with its scythe, and begin to imagine, to invent, possible solutions? Because there is no one to stand up, as did the Camus of '56 in such a stirring way, there is no one today able pronounce once more, in the midst of the struggle, those words of an impotence not quite powerless, those words of suffering that one last time continues to live in hope.... Hope in the face of the irrevocable pursuit of the hideous Gorgon, of fratricidal war (perhaps, in this procession of writers it is Camus who first felt the strange fissure involved in living in the very heart of a colonial war, a civil war, as a rending of the breast!). Yes, who will speak out once more, at the end of these years '93 and '94, already too heavily burdened with corpses, who will echo Camus:

"If I had the power to give voice to our solitude and anguish, would it be in that voice that I would speak to you now?"

But this "you" to whom it might be possible to speak, who can it now be? Myself, if I were to say "you," I would be speaking only to the dead, to my friends, my brothers of the pen.

Besides which, perhaps if I see myself plunging deeply into a past forty years old, it's because in the town of Algiers at the start of the year '57 the mechanics of violence and carnage correspond very largely to the schema practiced today: on one side as on the other, unleashers of death—on one side in the name of the law, but using mercenaries and hirelings, on the other in the name of a historical justice which is often ahistorical and transcendental, and thus incorporating both its illuminati and its "demons." Between these two extremes, from where the clash of arms is born, from where the daggers are drawn, there opens onto infinity a field on which the innocent fall—far too many ordinary people and a certain number of intellectuals.

<u>3</u>

The year '57. That "terrible year" was marked by the death of two heroes, two antithetical deaths, one phosphorescent, the other murky. One offering its light and its thirst for sacrifice, the other clouded by a tangle of lies attempting to change its nature. As for the two men, Larbi Ben M'Hidi and Abane Ramdane—one dying in March '57 in Algiers, at the hands of Massu's parachute troops, the other in the last days of December '57, strangled in Morocco, at the hands of his brothers—who can tell with what hope or with what despair their last breaths were taken?

On February 23rd, at dawn, parachutists burst into an apartment on Rue Claude Debussy, in the European quarter, and arrest Larbi Ben M'Hibi in his pajamas. They thought they were on the trail of Ben Khedda, another leader of the C.C.E. (Coordinating and Executing Committee). The game they trapped, however, was much more important. Unlike his colleagues on the Committee who had just left the capital to join up with the nearest *maquis*, and from there take refuge abroad, Ben M'Hidi—one of the nine historical leaders in charge of the armed groups in the capital—doesn't want to leave town. He simply gave up his usual hiding places, too near the Casbah wide open to security checks day and night.

Yacef Saadi was to recount that at one of his last meetings with the leader he had murmured, with his special seductive gentleness:

"I'd like to die in combat!... Before the end."

The photograph of his arrest in all the Algiers newspapers the following day shows him with hands chained, and a smile—not a smile of bravado, but one of inner certitude—lighting up his face, the fine features of a man of thirty-four. "In combat," he had prophesized for himself: he was first to endure ten days of interrogation by Bigeard and his men.

Twenty-eight years later, on November 1st, 1984, in the course of an interview specially granted to the Algerian paper Algérie-Actualité, *Bigeard was to declare that he had been "constrained, on orders from Paris, to hand over Larbi Ben M'Hidi, alive, to the Special Branch."*

And in fact, for ten days, Ben M'Hidi stood up under the extreme pressure of interrogation, insisting to Bigeard on his certainty of a final Algerian victory. The French colonel was impressed by the dignity of the man: defeated, but in no way broken.

On the tenth day then, March 4th, 1957, Bigeard had to agree to "Ben M'Hidi being transferred to another prison for administrative reasons." The services of Massu's Special Branch took over. What exactly happened in the course of that day of March 5th and the following night?

On March 6th, a Lacoste press release announced that Ben M'Hidi "had committed suicide by hanging himself with strips of material torn from his shirt." Massu, later, was to state that Ben M'Hidi, after a day of severe torture, "had hanged himself with electric cable, but was still breathing upon arrival at the Maillot hospital."... Two doctors from the hospital, however, declared that the prisoner had been dead on arrival, but without visible marks of injury.

So many contradictory versions make the thesis of suicide altogether suspicious. Bigeard, overwhelmed when faced with the body of the tortured man, supposedly had him buried with full honors and later insisted to the Algerian newspaper: "You must say that it was the Special Branch that did this!"

It wasn't a blunder. "On orders from Paris," Bigeard was later to say, wanting to safeguard his own honor.

From this point onwards torture is institutionalized in the French military machine. In '57 alone, the list lengthens: the disappearance of Maurice Audin, a Marxist academic from the faculty of Algiers, the "suicide" of Ali Boumendjel, a young Algerian lawyer thrown from a window in the course of his interrogation, and so many others less widely known.

In late March '57 General de Bollardière, Companion of the Liberation, protests publicly in *L'Express,* citing "the terrible danger," as he puts it, "that exists if we lose sight, on the false pretext of immediate necessity, of the moral values which, alone so far, have made our civilization and our army great." The general is sentenced to sixty days in prison.

Then the secretary general of the prefecture of Algiers, Paul Teitgen, Hero of the Resistance, veteran of Dachau where he had been tortured repeatedly, sends Lacoste, the governor, his letter of resignation: he cannot condone such practices, and he will refuse to have the Communist, Yveton, tortured, who was arrested in the act of planting a bomb. Yveton, condemned to death, was later to be executed in Barberousse.

It is also in '57 that Henri Alleg was to be "interrogated." His book *La Question (The Questioning),* published in '58, which gives a precise description of his own lengthy trials, along with the testimony of Servan-Schreiber, Pierre-Henri Simon, and several others, would help place the question of torture at the center of public debate in France:

Furthermore, the same production numbers are staged over and over: during the repression of the "Battle of Algiers" families first saw figures masked by a rough cloth bag over their heads with a hole at eye level, or sometimes with their face covered by a black hood, accompanying the security officers, and always the informer's finger stretched out: the tortured man who has broken down or the suspect who immediately gave up even his own brother, hiding his face, his identity, in black.

A funereal theater is hauntingly inscribed once more in the nights of fear.

Abane Ramdane, upon the announcement of Ben M'Hidi's phony suicide that stunned those Nationalists still in hiding (from Yacef Saadi and the young bomb-carrying girls, violence breaks out again, this time without quarter for the civilian population), Abane, traveling with his friends among the *maquis* of the Blida and Chréa regions, chooses to cross the border into Morocco.

From there he flies to Tunis, where he'll stay for six or seven months. He meets up again with Krim Belkacem (who's left the leadership of Kabylia to Amirouche) and Ben Tobbal, who had directed the resistance in the north of the Aurès after Zirout Youssef's death in combat. Along with Mahmoud Chérif and Ouamrane, with Boussouf who for the most part stays rooted in his fiefdom in Morocco, the colonels, who are now in the majority, go back on the decisions made at the Soummam Congress.

Abane opposes this development; he sticks by his principle of the primacy of the political over the military; his second rule—to give precedence to the leaders of the interior over those outside the country—he can no longer apply, since he himself is on the outside. But he relinquishes neither his fervor nor his trenchant use of words; his intransigence isolates him even from the moderates who owe to him, like Ferhat Abbas, their participation in this illusory collegiality. How might we keep alive the flame in the interior, how might we avoid the destruction of several thousand warriors by an army of what is now six hundred thousand men while the electrified barriers are raised? These are the only questions that preoccupy Abane. And he wears himself out denouncing in every possible way petty political ambitions and falsehoods. In short he wants to overturn the tactics of shadow and darkness.

It was to be in shadow and darkness that he would be killed, one winter's night, near Tétouan, at the end of December 1957.

4

Yes, now I see it clearly: Abane is a tragic hero because he goes to his death with his eyes open.

He knows, he senses in advance that the trap is being laid. "They won't dare!" he tells himself, not at all because he overestimates his own influence, but because he cannot yet quite believe that men who only yesterday were heroes, and had been for years, could change their spots and become mafia men. And yet it actually is he who in conversation with Ferhat Abbas (who as a friend advises him to "go and take a rest in Switzerland") declares with strange foreboding:

"Algeria is not the Orient where potentates exercise undivided power. We'll save our freedom against hell and high tide, even if we have to leave our skin behind!"

On December 25th, 1957, Abane Ramdane has his friend Mouloud Gaïd, with whom he has been staying since he arrived in Tunisia, drive him to the Tunis airport.

On the way the two men discuss the mission which Abane has been given: accompanied by Krim Belkacem and Mahmoud Chérif, he is to go to Morocco—via Rome and Madrid. Once there, joined by Boussouf who will be waiting for them, they are to try to settle directly with Sultan Mohammed V a legal dispute that has arisen between Chérif's army and the Algerian armed forces. Supposedly they are going to need no less than four leaders from the Central Committee to resolve this dispute.

Abane is tense, mistrustful: since the summer he has been isolated. He has been gradually excluded even from the meetings of the C.E.E. They authorized "a de facto surveillance over those he sees frequently." All they have left him is the newspaper, with Fanon, Boumendjel, Malek and El Mili: let him stay with his intellectual friends while Krim deals with defense on his own, and Boussouf with intelligence. And suddenly they call on him for a problem concerning the Maghreb?

Mouloud Gaïd manages to convince him that under these conditions he should turn back: it feels like a plot. What's more, no one has heard a word of this problem with the Moroccans. Boumendjel has made investigations: even His Majesty's Ambassador knows nothing about it!

They turn round. But hardly has he got back than Abane, increasingly tense, keeps repeating:

"I don't want them to think I haven't got the guts. I don't want to be diverted from my duty!"

He calms down, sets out for the airport again, although all the way on this second trip he admits to being gripped by a sense of foreboding. He stops Gaïd at the entrance to the airport. Before going to join those who are waiting for him in the V.I.P. lounge, he has time to murmur to his friend:

"I'm going to take a pistol with me to Boukkadoum's in Madrid. If by the 27th, 28th or 29th of December you haven't had a telegram from me saying: "I'm alright," then you must let Dr. Lamine Debaghine know!"

He starts to go. After hesitating, he comes back, takes a photograph out of his pocket which he offers to Gaïd: it is a photo of his wife Izza (they were married in secret the previous year in Algiers) with their son, then a baby a few weeks old. He finishes by saying:

"They'll arrive in Tunis soon. I'd like you to fetch them and watch over them!"

The three travelers—Krim, Mahmoud Chérif and Abane—arrive at the Tetuan Airport on December 27th, just before nightfall.

An Algerian witness who happens to be at the airport recognizes Abane, whom he will not see again. And Boussouf is there, with some of his men; a car drives off with them in the direction of Tangiers. Fairly soon, the driver turns onto a secondary road which leads to an isolated farm.

Just before leaving the airport, Boussouf has time to say, in an aside to Krim:

"There isn't a prison secure enough to guard Abane. I've decided on his physical liquidation!"

A heavy silence in the car. Might Abane be carrying a weapon, Abane who they say is never armed, even in the very heart of danger? Abane nevertheless alerted his friend Gaïd, from Madrid, according to the agreed code, saying that he has noticed several "odd things."

Abane's last thoughts in that car? He senses clearly enough that this three-day journey is about to end in a terrible confrontation—he alone against the three of them. But he refuses, right to the end, to believe that he is being led into a trap.

Hardly have they gone into the building together than six or seven waiting thugs, lurking beasts, throw themselves on Abane and pin him down. One of them hits him in the Adam's apple, then they drag him, already a sacrificial victim, into the next room. Boussouf, beside himself, follows and locks himself up with them.

The two others, it appears, make a show of moving forward to protest. It was only—one of them says, thus revealing that the plot was premeditated—a question of frightening Abane, then locking him up for a while. They were agreed on that, and Ben Tobbal who'd stayed in Tunis, had also decided on this "sanction." Not on murder!

Meanwhile, on the other side of the door, Abane is struggling. The colonels hear his death rattle... to the end.

Upon which Boussouf comes out, his face convulsed. And Krim's later comment:

"At that moment he had the face of a monster!"

Do the protestations again flare up, even though now they are futile? Krim, still following his own version, claims that Boussouf suddenly started to threaten *them*: and indeed the pack is still there, ready to be unleashed!

Mahmoud Chérif tells that from the very beginning of the violence, although unarmed, he put his hand in his jacket pocket to give the impression that he would be ready to defend himself.

Boussouf gradually calms down and they end up... going out to dinner in a restaurant in Tetuan!

Another version, contrary to that of Krim, speaks of the evening the three accomplices dined out: in the course of the meal someone is supposed to have come to let Boussouf know that the task had been accomplished.

According to this variant, Mahmoud Chérif still keeps his hand in his jacket pocket.

Clearly this less dramatic version is inconvenient for Krim insofar as it proves that the plot hatched in Tunis by the colonels included the possibility of murder. It could not have been a last minute initiative on the part of Boussouf alone!

Ferhat Abbas, still living in Montreux, in Switzerland, is informed of the murder that January by Mehri and Mahmoud Chérif.

He goes to Tunis at the beginning of February. In the course of a stormy meeting, Krim solemnly affirms:

"I'll take everything upon myself! I'll take responsibility for Abane's death. In my soul and in my conscience he was a danger to our movement: I have no regrets!

Then Boussouf in turn makes the same speech: he considers that by this liquidation he is certain of having saved the Revolution!

The gentle Ferhat Abbas is overwhelmed:

"Who made you judges?" he exclaims, leaving the room with Dr. Lamine Debaghine. "I resign!"

He was not to resign. Eight months later he returned as President of the first G.P.R.A., the Provisional Government of the Algerian Republic. This new structure, although merely a formal entity for the Algerian resistance, has the merit nonetheless of partially throttling the essentially military character assumed by the new powers that be. The 3 B's (Boussouf, Belkacem Krim, Ben Tobbal) constitute the triumvirate which was, *de facto*, to hold the reins until '62, and it is a blood pact— around the body of Abane—which both unites and divides them.

Whereas Krim would forget himself enough to say several times, in Berber, of Abane's murder: "*Ghasigh Itoudhaniw*," which means "I bitterly repent of it," Ben Tobbal, known as the Chinaman, the only survivor of that formidable trio, who admittedly had remained in Tunis to await there the accomplishment of the fatal action, was to conclude:

"Now that Abane has been liquidated, his blood will bar our way to power forever; it will be others who will seize it!"

He was predicting the final exit, in July 1962.

As for Ferhat Abbas, the most senior of the Nationalist leaders, who by his age, experience and training could have been the father and the moderator of all these plotters, he was to lay the following statement before them:

"Whatever you say and whatever you do"—and here Abbas speaks most directly to Krim, the only one of the nine historical leaders both alive and free—"there will always remain between us that bloody shadow!"

Abane, the sacrificial victim, a bloody shadow? Rather a giant shadow, the first specter of our independence.

Meanwhile the lies are woven and printed.

On May 29th, 1958, *El Moudjahid* in Tunis made the announcement, enclosed in a black border: "Abane Ramdane Dies on the Field of Honor!"

The story told is that since December '57 brother Abane had been on an important mission in the interior of the country. He had managed to pass through the enemy lines. "His mission was being carried out slowly but surely." Then there is mention of a violent clash between Algerian troops and those of the enemy. In the course of the fighting Abane was wounded. "For weeks we remained without news.... Alas, a serious hemorrhage must have proved fatal." Then followed biographical details of "one of Algeria's most valorous sons," etc.

The obituary notice, in these conventional terms, became yet another attempt to stifle not only the assassinated man, but his very ghost.

5

In the recent memoir of one of the fighters, one who was there from the beginning and remains true (a few do still exist, but they most often wall themselves in bitter silence), there is the report of a village scene full of bleak significance.

A funeral ceremony, as was so common during those thirty-three years. At this one, a few years after independence, Abane Ramdane was reinhumed in Azouza, his Kabylian village.

A microphone was set up in the middle of the tiny cemetery. The population of the village and surrounding countryside came in large numbers. Veteran *maquisards*, particularly from Districts III and IV made the effort. They were invited to speak one after another, as were a few distinguished personalities from the capital, who remembered Abane in dithyrambic terms without it being clear as to whether or not they had really known the hero.

As the speeches droned on, the audience fell silent, withdrew into itself. It was as though the real purpose of all the eloquence pouring forth was to bury deeper in the earth, alongside the corpse, the only question to be read in the eyes of those present: "How did our Abane Ramdane really die and, above all, why did you kill him?"

This was in the mid-sixties; Boussouf certainly was not there (from '62 onwards he had withdrawn from the political stage and its conflicts to immerse himself in the grayness of business life). Ben Tobbal must undoubtedly have been there, but he kept silent. And it was Krim Belkacem—after all, a man from the region—retaining, in spite of his corpulence, the stature of an old lion, who stood up in his turn, walked calmly to the microphone and, without remorse or unease, launched into a conventional eulogy of Abane Ramdane.

Then out of the semi-circle made up of the peasants present, so far apparently docile, attentively docile, stepped a young man. In a steady voice, full of contained anger, he interrupted Krim's speech, only exploding towards the end:

"Stop! Stop your perorations over my brother! You killed him yourselves, and now you dare to weep over his tomb! That's the last straw!"

(*Was his indignation expressed in that trenchant tone and was his
final anger cried in the Berber tongue?*)

Hubbub and commotion. A few, out of a sense of propriety, or so
they said, stepped in to calm down the hero's fuming brother.

"Let's just allow the ceremony to carry on in peace!" exclaimed one.

"In peace and in God's mercy," added another in support, this
time in Koranic terms.

Krim Belkacem, standing erect amidst the tombs, hadn't moved.
Hadn't turned round. In the renewed silence, he started up again, this
time more forcefully:

"I understand the pain suffered by Abane's relative," he declared
to all. "The dossier for this case is in the hands of the government. I
am asking for it to be reopened..." (there was a pause, then slowly he
added):

"I am not the only one involved in this business!"

The witness describing the scene, Ali Zaamoum, then writes: "It
sounded to me like an admission of guilt. I retained the fact that he
had said: 'I was not the only one!' I looked at the *Djurdjura* opposite, immense and mysterious, at those villages whose paths were
trodden by Lalla Fatma N'Summer, those landscapes richly laden
with history and I said to myself that something was rotten in our
revolution!"

The ceremony, in the cemetery at Azouza, followed its course
relentlessly.

One morning a few years later, Krim Belkacem—who had openly
opposed the power of Boumediene—was found lifeless in a hotel
room in Germany. Strangled in his turn.

Boumediene died at the end of 1978. In 1984, they built and dedicated a *Carré des Martyrs* in his honor in the El-Alia cemetery in Algiers.

On this occasion the body of Abane Ramdane had the right to a third tomb. For a third time the death of this man "fallen on the field of honor" was celebrated; there were probably more speeches, just as pompous as the others. This time ("this was the last straw," Abane's brother would have said), they buried him right next to… Krim Belkacem, his murderer, lying not far from the imposing tomb of Boumediene, the latter being in fact the murderer of the murderer.

Three heroes, among others; before them, the successive rulers in Algiers come to pay their respects every November 1st and renew the "November Oath."

Again Ali Zaamoum concludes bitterly:

"They buried the assassins and their victims together. They decorated them all and declared them officially 'Heroes of the revolution.' They granted themselves titles, ranks and medals quite shamelessly," and Ali, who at the age of twenty was one of the first of the November 1st, now protests: "If the November ideal could have been so shamelessly taken over, what about the rest?"

Hardly surprising that the revolt and anger, even deflected, even derailed, of today's "madmen of God" should be directed first and foremost against the cemeteries, against the tombs of the *chahids,* yesterday's sacrificial victims.

Above all, what can you say of those who continued to rule in the confusion of that hollow political theater? In their speeches they were to invoke the dead on every occasion—by dint of repeating "a million dead," they paid attention only to quantity, they, the survivors, in the pink of health, becoming more and more at ease year by year, gaining weight, complacency, space, nourishing their bank accounts,

some turning towards a conservatism, ostentation, lukewarm religiosity, others towards a moral delicacy which could only become
more and more hypocritical.... And thus would develop the carica-
ture of a past in which sublimated heroes and fratricidal murderers
were to be mingled in an hazy blur.

How then can we get out of this mire—in what language, in what
aesthetic form of denunciation and anger—how can we give an
account of these changes? The only question which should have
taken root in the heart of a living Algerian culture continued to
remain a gaping hole, a dead eye—with just two exceptions in the
theater: in French the farcical, ironic foresight of Kateb Yacine, and,
in a witty and vigorous dialectal Arabic, the dramatic works of
Abdelkader Alloula, which even now remain so fresh.

Yet both, as I write, are dead. And we miss them.

Who among us, in the whole of the past thirty-five years, has thought
of writing "A Tomb of Abane Ramdane": in Berber, in French or in
Arabic? Occasionally you would see a statement by a political com-
mentator, a historian or a polemicist.... Almost never was the symbol
of our amnesia illuminated.

And so Abane's ghost continues alone along the path; yet in the
desolate countryside, I know, he sometimes meets writers of this land,
dead men lightened of their loads, their pens hardly set down.

PROCESSION 2

I

Jean Sénac, dying in 1973 in the heart of the Algiers Casbah, never knew, sought all his life, but never knew who his father was. But who, in the tangled Algeria of this last century has really known a father? Named him? Loved him?

Jean Sénac died in that pitch-black night of August 30th, 1973 at 2 Rue Elisee-Reclus; he was probably killed by a one–night stand, a robber, or perhaps a police spy.

His weekly poetry broadcast on the Algerian Francophone radio had been suppressed a year earlier for reasons which aren't clear.

Some biographers, noting that the first poet killed in Algeria—in the between-the-wars Algeria, and so in peacetime Algeria—was all the same a *pied-noir* from Beni-Saf, let it be understood that already, hardly more than ten years after independence, the country was reneging on its highly touted tradition of openness and pluralism.

It may also be true that Jean Sénac, who signed his poems and missives with a five-pointed sun, lived his loves—of his native land, of life, of boys—in a dazzlement which cast a suddenly violent shadow over a society in which homosexuality, however omnipresent avoids speaking its name.

Jean sometimes liked to be called Yahia el-Ouahrani: Jean l'O-ranais died of his own truth, spoken, written, sometimes cried out loud.

As the poet Salah Guemriche puts it:

Hear me, people of the streets, when I tell you
Yahia was not assassinated
So much as completed.

So all the poets present in Algiers expressed the warmth of their feelings by offering a funeral wreath to their friend: Djamal Amrani, Laghouati, Djaout, Sebti, and many others beside, their gaze pure and their hearts full of giving. Two of their number were later to be struck down in their turn: Tahar Djaout in full daylight, one sunny morning, and Youssef Sebti during a long painful night, at the other end of Algiers.

Thus Jean Sénac, alas, was to be at the head of a chain of poets whose song was stifled.

Three months before his death, he wrote:

I have loved too much. This evening
Space reduces being
to the breaking of a reed!

2

A spring day in 1978: this time I'm living again in Algiers.

A friend goes to visit the novelist Malek Haddad, who has just been taken to the hospital and for whom the doctors seem to have given up hope; he's probably living his last days; the cancer attacking him was turning out to be ferocious.

On an impulse, I suggest I go with the friend. Soon afterwards I find myself sitting by Malek's bed, chatting cordially. Through the open window bright sunlight floods the hospital room.

Sometimes writers die before they die. Yes, sometimes they die an inner death: sometimes it takes them (in any country where there are publishers, readers, critics, and literary prizes), takes them like an illness.

Turn away and be silent. Look no more in the booksellers' windows, and be silent. Turn away from a table with inkpot and typewriter, avoid a friend coming towards you on the pavement (he'll say for sure: "So, what about your next book?), walk alone in the forest, or in town drift from one bar to the next, rush into the arms of a first lover, a second, let the word find a rhythm for itself within the self, a cavalcade, a murmur, listen to that voice, that strange voice for the self alone, from where does it rise, whose voice is it in truth?

Do not write, let the emptiness spread out, weigh it in your hands, let it calm you. Let yourself live. Let yourself be lulled by the anthem of time, everyday phrases, drown in the chit-chat—children cry in the night, outside the bustling crowd, madmen in the plazas mouth their soliloquies, beggars pass the hat in quest of silence...

No longer write. Be silent? Speak to be silent.

In Algiers, as everywhere, why do writers die before they die? At thirty or at fifty. In the Algeria of the seventies, I remember, nationalized oil reassures everyone, the common people, the civil servants, the veteran heroes, the militants who have settled down and been promoted: the whole country is frozen, apart from the women who are making lots of babies, more and more of them.

The writers flicker out, like lamps: often enough surrounded by honors.

I have described this anemia, and may Malek Haddad in his paradise forgive me! Here I wish to recall simply the death of a man—one of fine presence and elegant manners, a spirit quieted, they tell me, thanks to a good wife, a recently born son and, as of late, daily practice of Islamic prayer; Malek felt that he was in safe harbor, so to speak.

When some of my Marxist friends made ironic comments on his ineffectiveness as Minister of Culture, I would attest to the good nature of the man. I had only one argument, which at the time I believed:

"In this country," I would say, "name one person who, after being entrusted with public office, didn't immediately use that power to cause harm to some adversary or other, in the name of God knows what rivalry!... But not Malek Haddad. He may not wield much power. But at least *he* doesn't abuse what power he has."

I knew that he loved the *chaabi* musicians with their Arab-Andalusian repertoire in the dialect of the common people and their ironic and lascivious poetry. He must have found his lost roots in that music.

That was when they told me the doctors' verdict.

"In fact," explained one of his women friends, "he had a warning two or three years ago. He had an operation: it was lung cancer. They opened him up. They closed him up again. They told him he could go home. He thought he was cured.... There was a two year remission. He's been in pain for three months. Since then his wife has known that the end is on its way, as do his friends and relations. He's quite reassured: the professor in charge of his wing of the hospital is one of his best friends! Malek doesn't ask any questions. It's as though, with childlike faith, he's entrusted his fate to those who love him. And, he's a loveable man!" sighed his friend finally.

"A decent man, it's true!" I said dreamily.

Already in those days we had so few of them!

Malek Haddad wrote two collections of poems, four novels, one essay, all work between 1956 and 1961. In five years.

Leaving Paris in 1958, he traveled all over the world: the Union of Asian Writers, the Pan-African Congress. Everywhere he spoke in the name of Algerian writers, of the Algerian revolution: he did so, I think, with fire and in good faith.

As at that time he still kept his old habit of blithely going off on binges and sprees, one day he sent a telegram from Karachi, or Indonesia or China, I can't remember which, to his publisher in Paris, who happened to be the same as mine. A very long telegram full of flights of nationalist and third-world rhetoric, and finishing with a diatribe against French imperialism! So why send it to René Julliard? Clearly, in the middle of an evening of song and dance, it must have been the only address in Paris he could remember.... The inflammatory telegram landed on René Julliard's desk in Paris (Julliard who was to die four years later, on the very day of Algerian Independence).

Some time later I was coming back from Tunis to take my exams at the Sorbonne, and I stopped in to say hello to Julliard, who with a troubled look showed me the telegram.

"Why send it to me?"

I smiled. I didn't know what to say. From the other end of the world, Malek Haddad, like a schoolboy, was playing a role, was enjoying playing it.

Nearly twenty years later, in that month of May '78, while I was sitting opposite the sick man, our three-way conversation was nourished, not by these Franco-Algerian ambiguities, but rather by the particular complexity of relations between men and women in Algeria. And, to my surprise, it was on Malek Haddad's own initiative.... Now I say to myself that he could foresee that his end was near, and that he was trying to say goodbye to me in his own way.... He undoubtedly wanted to show me, at least once, his friendship... or his sympathy, I suppose, or rather a vague sense of unease, not only in relation to me perhaps, but also in relation to the other women of that land that he had not dared to approach!

"What do you think, Djaffer?" began Malek Haddad, speaking to our friend, but with his eyes fixed on me, "What do you think of this scene: in the middle of the Algerian war, in Paris, two Algerian writers are sitting in the same room, both signing the press copies of their novel. It lasts three or four hours.... Well, you'd hardly believe it, they don't exchange a single word!"

The friend was probing me with his eyes. I had completely forgotten the scene in question: it was true, I was twenty-one, signing the copies of my second novel. They'd taken me into a long gloomy room. At the far end a novelist was set up—about thirty—writing dedications in his first novel, *La Dernière Impression*.

The publicist who was with me told me, very quietly, the name of the author and the title of his book. She waved goodbye and left.

Installing myself at the other end, I plunged into my task. I knew, of course, that he had to be from my own country, or at least from the Maghreb. Only once did I glance at him. I must have kept my nose in my books for an entire three hours. What could be more natural for me, then: I would only speak to someone (if it was a man) if I had been introduced, or if he came up to introduce himself, whether king or beggar.

As Malek, in his bed, was evoking our encounter, gradually taking on more of a tone of reproach, the scene I had forgotten was reconstituting itself in my mind. I reacted with a hint of irony:

"Of course," I explained to the friend who was there, "it was

Malek and myself, exactly twenty years ago, at the Julliard publishers!" (I smiled at Malek.) "Tell me Malek, during all those hours, why didn't *you* come over to me? It was up to you to introduce yourself: you were older than me, and after all, you are a man!"

He didn't reply. Seemed to dream for a moment.... Had I annoyed him so much and so thoughtlessly?

Malek remained encased in a kind of melancholy, whereas this time our friend laughed openly. I realized how strangely unreal this first silence between us had been, that day in Paris in 1958: it wasn't only my stiffness (or rather that outward distance quite naturally assumed), but also the paralysis which had overcome the young Malek Haddad: he hadn't dared come towards me with outstretched hand, offering his book to receive mine in exchange.... Why that ossification in both of us?

In any case, he suddenly reawakened the memory of that non-meeting, whereas for some time I had been coming across him by chance in the streets of Algiers or in the house of friends; our relations henceforth seemed to be cordial, on the level of everyday courtesy.

How was the rest of my visit? I remember the brightness of the sunlight, the confident, suddenly almost gay tone of the sick novelist. Djaffer and I had drawn closer to his bed. A nurse came, and I can still see the four of us laughing. Standing up, near the window, I was saying to myself that I ought to leave, but I was lingering: a friendly warmth was passing between us.

I leaned towards the invalid, my heart wrenched ("Shall I see him again?" I asked myself.) I gave him a brave smile. I kissed him on the cheeks. I said, to bring things to an end, gaily, to veil my emotion:

"Did you notice, Malek, that since I came in I've been using the informal *tu* with you... for the first time.... It's because I completely forgot you were Minister of Culture!"

All three of us laughed. I abruptly turned my back. I went out first.

In the corridor I hurried. Outside, at the door of the building, facing the courtyard and its chestnut trees, I leaned my back against the wall. My heart was beating.

To tell the truth I have to say that it was the sun—so bright, so vertiginous—that assailed me with a kind of violence. The truth was that in an extraordinarily egoistic way my heart was beating with the acute understanding that I, in that instant standing up and not lying down, ready that day to wander around the town, and not nailed to a hospital bed, I was going to live. I was alive, I wasn't going to die, at least not that day, not perhaps the following day, nor the day after that!...

I took deep breaths, eyes closed, to attenuate my dizziness, and in my inner depths there formed beads of mournful compassion for the man: so he was going to depart, so it was from the regions of darkness that Charon's barque was unceasingly preparing to come to fetch him!

Djaffer, who had come to join me, stared at me in silence. He took my arm and kept it all the while leading me out of the hospital.

"You did well to come, Assia, he was really moved!"

"It's only now," I said, "that I feel that I'm having a conversation with him!... What a strange country," I added in the car, "what a harsh land. Ten or so, maybe twenty or so writers live in this town, and each one of them is lost in solitude!"

Malek Haddad died on June 2nd, 1978, at the age of fifty. His father taught French in Constantine. The day after his wedding, he had pressed his wife (Malek's mother) into lifting the traditional veil.

Shortly before the Algerian war, Malek found himself a student in Aix-en-Provence. There he met Kateb Yacine, the painter Issiakhem, and other young politically engaged compatriots.

He aspired to be a poet, under the influence of Louis Aragon, who praised his first collection of poems: *Le Malheur en danger.* Someone told me that his brief voluntary exile in the Libyan desert had influenced his vocation even more forcefully.

So what do I seek in unreeling this procession of the dead? (I am seized with anxiety, perhaps I shall be gripped by the violent desire to cross over there, to pass in my turn over to the other side, also unburdened and joyful, evanescent like them!) Perhaps they will draw me to them, since sometimes I have the dull heavy thought that there remains nothing around me, around us, but a blind hatred, of which we are neither the targets, nor, evidently, the source, we are there by mishap.

Nothing around us. You spoke of Algeria? The Algeria of yesterday's suffering, that of the night of colonialism, that of the mornings of fever and trance? You said this land, this country: no, a dream of sand, no, a populous caravan that faded from sight, no, a Sahara all flooded with oil and mud, a Sahara betrayed...

An Algeria of blood, of streams of blood, of bodies decapitated and mutilated, of stupefied, staring childlike eyes.... In the middle of this gallery of death I am seized by the desire to put down my pen or my brush and go off to them, to join them: to bathe my face in their blood (that of the victims of assassination), to rend my joints with them, the ones mowed down on the road by a car, and as for those who died in their beds, in the circle of family farewells, I would not want to be like Taos the priestess, reigning and chanting to brave death: no, rather, to avoid shrieking out my farewell, cover my mouth with both hands, rise up myself—myself not my song—hurl myself alive and vibrant, plunge into the immense Ganges of desolation, of putrefaction, of water.

To join them, that is the temptation. I might as well stop short the account if it becomes the cord of a future garrote for me. I stand up straight, here on the other side: facing them, but not with them. They left me against

*my will. I remain here, and if I turn my head and think I see the desert,
then I am deceiving myself, blinding myself, deluding myself!*

*I simply no longer see Algeria. I am simply turning my back on my
native soil, on my birth, on my origin.*

*I am simply discovering the whole of the earth, the other countries,
the many histories: too bad if, for the moment, beings, trees, cats suddenly seem to me flat, squashed down on the surface, almost coming out of
the pages of a children's cartoon book. Too bad if I don't quite believe in
this variability, this rebirth.*

*I simply live again elsewhere; I surround myself with elsewhere and
my pulse continues to beat. And I regain the desire to dance. I laugh
already. I cry as well, straight afterwards, troubled to note that laughter
is returning. What, I'm getting over it! In my own way, I forget.*

*I forget the blood and I forget the murderers. How wide the world!
As wide as my heart. I felt that I was pacing a dark kingdom where gradually Ariana, Oriana and even Antigone, Fatima as well—"the mother
of the two Hosseins"—were going to help drive away the monsters and
their sinister fabulations.*

*It's the darkness that drove me away. I saw you, you my friends, on
the other side: your writing (which carried your voices) I knew to be the
thread in the labyrinth.... There is no longer even a labyrinth... You, still
over there, and I, expelled from the desert.*

*I am inexplicably pulled elsewhere. I see myself elsewhere; you follow
me a moment from afar; you promise me not to fade away.*

*I am there with no native land, your voices alone cross the frontier,
first you three, as when I was asleep in California; then the others from
the first quartet, and those of the second. How long will your voices sus-
tain me, guide me, thrust me forward?*

*I turn my eyes: the landscape broadens, multiplies. I wished it so, I
shall go live in Egypt, then in China... And I shall find once more friends*

and companions, sisters vanished.... Their strength; their gaiety, their presence that fills the absence. Very close to me, they come towards me.

Thanks to them above all, I want to continue to write to drown my eyes in sky: Algeria is a brilliant or dying star, not the whole firmament!... Go on? I should say, like one of Beckett's last characters: "I go on... I can't go on. I go on because I can't go on."

3

The third is a child cherished by the gods, and at first sight that might seem surprising. After all, that particular writer was to die older than anyone else on the list, at the age of seventy-one. And yet I see him so young, his slim silhouette, refined, almost sculptured, his face lit up by a sly smile; at the same time by a hint of shyness.... Such was my last meeting with him two months before he disappeared, or so it seems.

He left happy. For some years—I had been glimpsing it gradually in our few meetings in the neighborhood (for he was a friend "from the neighborhood")—for some years I had been realizing it more precisely: in the last five or six years of his life he had finally regained his earlier youthfulness, and he deserved it.

That particular morning I saw him from afar. In a deserted and sunlit street in the city's heights. Once I'd reached him, I made a gentle little pout.

"So you don't recognize me?"

He recognized me. I had cut my hair too short. I cannot recall what he said to me. He and I, face to face in the morning sun. I was floating in a state of visual bliss: I had arrived the previous evening; it was December. I had left Europe's grayness behind and was rediscovering the light once again!

"Before I saw you in the distance, I was walking with my head in the clouds. How lovely this city is, iridescent like this! I can't get enough of it: as if it were the first time! I never tire of the façades or the balconies of the houses, and especially not of the sky!...."

He smiled at me. I didn't dare tell him that, as I watched him approach, I was envying his ability to grow slimmer as he aged: an ever–narrowing silhouette.

"Come to visit us," he said as we were parting, "and you will experience one of the most beautiful views of the city!"

"It's a promise," I told him, impulsively, "I'll come. I'll phone you one of these days and I'll come."

He lived not far from my father's house. I left him to continue walking, immersed in the glow of the morning's well–being. I went on, head high.

This was in December '88. I think that I then made a rather serious comment to myself: "How odd! Every time I meet Mouloud Mammeri, which has been going on since...before '62—since '60, in Morocco already!—no matter where, in my neighborhood or elsewhere, we just joke around, he and I, we laugh like two schoolchildren!"

Suddenly I found something was lacking: a frost seemed to seep into our words suddenly.... A woman and a man in Algeria, both writers moreover, what do they say to each other? They should have so much to say to each other and, precisely for that reason, they say nothing!

Early in February I was back in Algeria. The desire for a truthful con-versation—especially because I couldn't manage to forget the autumn of the six hundred dead!—rose up in me again:

"Talk, perhaps we could really talk, at least among writers?" I said to a publisher friend in Algiers.

I mentioned my meeting with Mammeri:

"It's not the first time he's invited me!" I remarked, "and it's not for the view of Algiers that I'd like to go and visit him... To talk, to talk just a few of us together... about everything that's brewing these days!"

I explained to him the drawback of being a woman in this country:

"I would really like to approach my fellow writers at least," I sighed, "but I don't see myself making the first move, for appearances' sake!"

My publisher friend was a good intermediary; his decision was made:

"I'll come and get you within the next few days! In the meantime, I'll phone Mammeri. We'll have a friendly get-together, at my place or his!"

I suggested seeing whether Kateb Yacine might not be able to join us: a few months earlier in Brussels I'd noticed that the October drama had left him voiceless.

"Let's comfort each other a little," I said hopefully, "and just for once let's forget protocol!"

My friend called me back not long thereafter:

Mammeri has just left for Morocco for a colloquium!... He'll be back in a week. If you're still here, we'll all get together then, just as you'd wished!"

Mouloud Mammeri chose to reach Morocco by road rather than plane.

Malika, a friend's sister who worked with him, had spoken to him on the phone the evening before his departure:

"Is that really a smart idea, Da LMouloud?"

"I know that route so well, my car is in good shape and these February days are so beautiful!"

"But," Malika insisted, "people here are so careless on the road! Be very careful, Da LMouloud!"

He laughed.

"I can still hear his laugh, the laugh of a young man!" she moaned much later.

"Come now, don't worry about me!" Mammeri answered, and then, after a silence, impish as ever, he added: "You know perfectly well that I'm immortal!"

He could have lingered in Oudja. Everyone wanted to see him: his Moroccan friends, journalists, and even an American friend, a professor close to him. They promised each other to get together in Algiers a little later for an interview.

Suddenly Mammeri was in a hurry. He wanted to get back on the road. He said that he would stop in Oran; and then perhaps in Sidi Bel Abbes for a longer time.

He rushed everywhere he went. He was alone on the road, the road of his adolescence—he had driven it the first time when he was fifteen and had gone to join his paternal uncle, friend and advisor to King Mohammed V. He was also reliving his happy return of July '62 (he had been forced to leave Algiers in '57, just barely escaping the legionnaires who were coming to arrest him in El-Biar). When he returned to his country, independent at last, elation had carried him down this same road—and now it all blends in his memory, including the recent delight, the crowds that had come together to hear him speak on behalf of Berber language and culture, on behalf of Si Mohand. So it had been these last few months, in Oran, in Aïn el-Hammam (where they presented him with a burnoose), in Bejaia in January where only the stadium was large enough for the thousands who had come to hear his lecture on Berber culture! And then the demonstration in Oudja with its Maghrebian warmth... Was he about to experience a repeat performance? Mouloud Mammeri wondered. No, he remarked modestly, he was just reliving the earlier visits.

He reflected on the lines he had written and sent off before he left to the conference of the Berber Cultural Movement that was held last February 10th:

"Recognizing Berber culture is the decisive test of democracy in the Maghreb."

Mammeri was in a hurry, yes. He didn't stop. Straight into the dark night that soon enfolded Aïn-Delfa, "the spring of bitter laurels."

The night of Saturday, the 25th of February 1989, after two or three weeks of premature spring weather—and worried farmers already fearing a season of drought—storms burst loose over central Algeria. I remember that night, the storm breaking, very specifically: I was supposed to leave Algiers the next morning. When I felt the suddenly chilly morning, I decided to delay my departure long enough to have dinner at the house of some teacher friends of mine that evening.

Dalila, the hostess who had gone down to buy the bread she had earlier forgotten, returned totally upset:

"Mouloud Mammeri died in a car crash last night: I just heard the news on the radio at the bakery!"

Mouloud Mammeri is driving a 205 ("a young man's car," Tahar Djaout would say later) between Aïn-Delfa and El-Khemis. It is about eleven at night; it's raining very hard. A 504 taxi is behind him, rather close. The two cars drive along like this for some ten kilometers.

At a curve, Mammeri is surprised by blinking lights from a stopped truck. He slams on the brakes; the taxi that has also just come around the bend crashes into the 205. Mammeri's car, pushed to the right, heads straight into a tree.

Wounded and unconscious, Mammeri is taken quickly to the nearest hospital in the area. In the emergency room he is admitted under his given name, Mohammed Mammeri. There are so many Mohammeds and quite a few Mammeris.

Nobody was able to say when exactly, in the course of that night or perhaps at the break of day of Sunday, the 26th of February, Mouloud Mammeri breathed his last.

His wife and daughter, notified by the hospital in the morning, came to identify him; they were the ones to inform them that this was Mammeri the writer.

Tahar Djaout, in many ways the closest literary descendant of the deceased, in a *Letter to Da LMouloud* published soon thereafter, stated, with gentle humor as was his wont:

"The evening that your death was abruptly and crudely announced on television, I couldn't help noticing—despite my unspeakable grief—that it was the second time your name was mentioned: the first time was to insult you when, in 1980, a shamefully libelous campaign had been unleashed against you, and now this second time, nine years later, to inform us of your passing.

"Your country's television had no footage of you to show us: it had never filmed you, it had never let you speak."

In Taourit-Mimoun, two hundred thousand people, a human tide, were present at the funeral.

A film of it shows children, women, and old peasants charging down the mountain paths, rushing to get to Beni-Yenni to honor the remains of Da LMouloud.

I repeat and believe it firmly: he was cherished by the gods, he who went to be reunited with the high mountain, "the one where I was born," he used to say to Jean Pélégri and would add: "in the splendor of her nudity."

He is indeed perhaps the only one on this list of my fellow writers who did not suffer an "untimely death!" My impression was confirmed before the smiling shadow fading into the rocks—Djurdjura's shadow and at the same time that of our language!...

The last months and weeks before his trip to Morocco—that ultimate and exalted "crossing"—Mammeri is completely immersed again in an intimate dialogue with Cheikh Mohand,or Lhocine; in the latter's language and by rereading his spiritual writing, happiness for Mammeri was felt on several planes. (That, it seems to me, is the origin of the aura that surrounded him his last year, that literally transformed this writer who was all too readily taken for a "man of letters," whose culture and refinement were praised, and whose caution and withdrawal were sometimes lamented, because in April '80, in fact, with fiery and romantic thrust, he could have taken the full leadership of the Berber cultural revolution, which he had set in motion, after all.)

During those nine years, Mammeri is inwardly more and more imbued with the strength of language, with its shimmer and its torment—the language of our ancestors that, step by step, sculpts his slow dialogue with his great predecessor—words restored, every inch of the way, reconstructed, brought back upstream, to the source—their language, that of the two of them.

In fact, a dialogue between a son—Mammeri—and his father in poetry, Cheikh Mohand, or Lhocine. Da LMouloud, too, exactly one century later, goes on a pilgrimage: and he warns us, casually:

"Most pilgrims," he wrote, remembering the history of those

mass movements at the end of the nineteenth century, in which the grandmother of Jean and Taos Amrouche herself participated, "most pilgrims come for a pious visit.... A small number seek wisdom and beautiful precepts (*ad-awin*)."

Of course, Mammeri belongs to this small number: he drinks of the source, not at all out of some mysticism that might have come to him in belated vapors to soften the rough edges of age—we've said it over and over again: Mammeri, in the decade of the eighties, does not drift; he grows stronger, his sharp, scathing pen resonates.

Mammeri does not grow old; he moves upstream, he flows, he glides (that is what I saw in that last encounter, that sunny December morning in Algiers, and if I had then known him to be mortal, I am sure that I would have freed myself of my rigid "good manners," I would have embraced him, kissed him...).

Confronted with Cheikh Mohand, or Lhocine, Mammeri discovers the poet—the sage and the poet—in the very instant the word appears, the poem unfolds.

Nabile Farès expresses it perfectly in his homage to Mammeri: "Earlier the poem was Word—*Awal*—a word within a language aspired to; inside; a word forgotten or gone astray, which the language regains, a rift, a margin, ravines or heights so distant or so negligible—Precipice-word; Forgotten-word."

In the novelist's last quest—research, listening, and writing—Mouloud Mammeri enthusiastically reconstructs the linguistic as well as the spiritual development of the very popular saint of Great Kabylia from 1870 until his death in 1901. The finished work, which Mammmeri wanted to publish both in French and in Tamazirt [the Berber word for its own language] was going to have the title: *Le Don souverain* [Sovereign Gift]: throughout his life it had been the object of his own pursuit, his Grail.

"The ability to create, apparently from nothing, is the Cheikh's sovereign gift. It is what sets him apart, something so remarkable that it seems miraculous."

And Mammeri patiently set about retracing the fragile path, the narrow and uncertain passage, the secret thread that links, separates, links up again, traces and leaves uncertainty, the trace between the virgin territory of the oral and the soil, hardened too soon, of the written: for it is no longer just a question of Tamazirt—whatever the most beautiful and the most ancient of languages may be—it is a question of what makes the secret emerge for all people, the secret and the effort and the dark, of what is emphasized between gaze and voice, and the hand that follows or flies off between gaze and voice, it is a question of the wing of the word, its translucence, it is a question for all people...

And there is Da LMouloud resubmerging himself in the surge of words of the old man, who lived a hundred years before him but in the same region, facing the same high mountain "in the splendor of her nudity."

"Thus," he wrote, "inspiration spurts forth from the moment. It seems to start from a kind of irrepressible urge, sometimes dictated by formal prompting. When piercing the meaning, you quickly notice that what had appeared at first to be pure wordplay is in reality the harvest of a sure and considered reflection or else of a sudden vision.... Hence, the special stamp of the Cheikh's teaching. He has reached the stage of thought gushing forth, of maieutics, that which is determined by the oral."

In *Sovereign Gift*, Mammeri mentions the death on the 8th of October, 1901 of this Berber poet-saint: a Tuesday, in the middle of the day, Cheikh Mohand, or Lhocine, gives up his spirit at the end of a long illness. Mammeri recounts it; he describes how greatly the news disturbs the region, the country; he recalls the processions of men and women coming from everywhere on the Taqqa road.

On the road of Beni-Yenni, thousands of men and women come from every corner and, eighty-eight years later, it is their turn to bury Mouloud Mammeri.

4

In that same period, early in March 1989, Kateb Yacine discovers that he is ill. He is in France; he has left Paris where he had received a major French prize the year before. His youngest son, an adolescent, is with him.

He no longer enjoys spending time in Paris: his friend and hostess, the most warmly devoted Jacqueline Arnaud had died the previous winter, practically collapsing in the poet's arms as she served him tea. Yacine plans to settle in Provence to write which amounts to his turning his back on the Algerian land.

She trembled and fell back into a trance; the earthquakes are returning, he, the poet knows it, he feels it—even without hashish-induced reveries in the room above the ravine of the Rummel, of Cirta, in the dances of Sidi MciD.

He knows it, he feels it: the black years, the violent years are returning, the Circle. Had he not ululated incessantly on the subject of that damned Circle: he, the poet, feels it!

But he is also weary, he can't go on anymore, he is turning his back on the Algerian land, on the imprisoned mother, on Nedjma who's gone. He goes away, he wants to. Suddenly the words return, a circle of birds of prey. Years of savagery?...

He, the poet, is weary: he falls silent, is stretched to the limit. He is leaving, even if the words and the birds of prey are returning!

In Algiers I met Ali Zaamoum who shared with me his wish:

"Next November 1st, I plan—and it will be my great pleasure— to hold festivities in my village. You know, Assia, that it is there that the preparation for the 1st of November 1954 actually began. I would like to start a festival there with two guests: Kateb Yacine and you. Will you accept?"

"I would be honored," I answered, first and foremost out of friendship for Ali.

I promised to stay in the village for a few days afterwards.

"You can learn Berber from our women!" Ali declared.

The 1st of November '89 came: early in the morning, Ali Zaamoum rushed off to the Algiers airport. A special plane, sent by the Algerian authorities, was bringing the body of its greatest poet home. Kateb Yacine had died on the 28th of October in Grenoble of leukemia, which had conquered him in just six months.

Strange coincidence, a first cousin of Yacine's, Mustapha Kateb (who had been the inspiration for one of the heroes of *Nedjma* and who was a first rate theater organizer of a sort of theater worlds apart from the work of Yacine) had died on the 29th of October in a hospital in Marseilles.

So the charter plane was bringing back the two bodies, cousins who hadn't spoken in years. On this final journey home, a woman in mourning had traveled with the bodies: another cousin, one whose beauty and aura, as a young girl, had been the muse for Kateb Yacine's heroine, the very real Nedjma whom the poet had loved as an adolescent, his first love from which he had never truly recovered.

At the airport, Ali Zaamoum observes the growing crowd. A room has been prepared. Officials are getting settled—ministers and top civil servants—and make themselves available to a group of journalists.

Disoriented for a moment, Ali, Yacine's friend of thirty years, notes that the funeral show has not only invaded the site of the dead *chahids*, martyrs buried and reburied; this time, the cultural field—the body of the purest of writers—too, becomes a pretext for graveside eloquence!

"They have never read a single line of the poet's work! When he was alive, they hardly dared to come near him, were afraid to greet him, facing the very real risk of receiving insults in return!" Ali says to himself bitterly, as he glances a last time at these characters in three-piece suits, then turns his back. His tall, thin silhouette moves away.

He goes back to Ighil-Imoula, his village: that is where Kateb will remain alive, especially today on this first day of November.

At the same moment, in Paris, I listen to a friend speak at length of Kateb, evoking him as he was during these last two years, trying to console herself, she who was the last woman to have loved him.

So often, and too easily really, Kateb Yacine was compared either to Rimbaud (like him, his luminous work was accomplished twenty-five years before his death) or to François Villon. Naturally, his Marxist friends preferred to compare him to the poet Mayakovsky. Not that Kateb had killed himself, no; but like the Russian poet he became disillusioned by everyday life and Algeria, and this more than anything else was what crushed him.

Let us first reinstate Kateb—it is the final moment—on his own soil.

He, Yacine, appears to me at the very moment that he is going to die as a brotherly shadow of the other great poet, Si Mohand, or M'hand, the most popular poet of Kabylia during the last thirty years of the past century. He died early in this century, in 1906, just a little over sixty years old.

More than twenty years later, Kateb Yacine was born in Eastern Algeria, destined amazingly for almost the same fate, as if inspired by the same angel. The story goes that by the edge of a spring an angel asked Si Mohand: "Choose: write verse and I shall speak or else speak and I shall write verse!" and they say that Si Mohand chose to speak!—and so the angel of precocious inspiration seems to have had a second encounter: "Speak and I shall write verse!"

Intertwining the two lives would not be a temptation without pertinence: such an early predestination, birth in a family of letters, but ruined and dispersed by the tragedy of Algerian history. (At the insurrection of 1871, Si Mohand sees his father shot, his uncle deported, the family possessions impounded; similarly, Yacine first has a happy childhood with a father who works in Muslim law and a mother who is a poet, but in 1945 his whole family is crushed by the repression of Sétif and of Guelma and he himself, an adolescent of fifteen, is imprisoned. After this breakup, he cannot continue his studies, his sick mother is hospitalized, and the early death of his father leaves him with heavy family responsibilities).

Both Kateb Yacine and Si Mohand are destined to be poet-wanderers their whole lives. "Lover of wide spaces and freedom, he goes where his star takes him": thus says Feraoun of Si Mohand, who was fond of sweet wine and absinthe, whose *isefras*—poems with a set form—sang only of love or the disappointment of love or of drunkenness, but always with a touch as sharp as steel. A tireless walker, Si Mohand never stopped traveling back and forth between Kabylia, the region of Bône and Tunisia.

Yacine, at seventeen, has a collection of poems published and, at eighteen, goes to Paris to give a lecture on the emir Abdelkader. Like Si Mohand he is immersed in the Berber language, but having studied classical Arabic in his uncle's religious school, the *zaouïa*, Kateb is between two languages from the start: his writing in French flows alongside his maternal Arabic.

Starting with the publication in 1956 of his masterpiece, *Nedjma*, Yacine's popularity, both in Algeria and Europe, brings him acclaim everywhere he goes. His popularity increases his roaming: in the U.S.S.R., Vietnam, Germany, Italy, as well as in independent Algeria. He returns, rather quickly leaves again, then settles there not long afterwards in 1970. More than thirty years go by, in which his nomadic existence expresses both his need for oxygen and the strong ties that bind him, for at times he aspires to nothing so much as settling down and writing in a stable environment.

"He scatters his *isefras*, his poems, like a farmer sows his field," Feraoun states, still on the subject of Si Mohand, about a hundred of whose poems were fortunately put to paper by Boulifa, the man of letters, even before the poet's death. The same is true for Kateb, in the abundance of his inspiration, in his carelessness with preservation (with him it is the fever of writing, throwing things down on the blank page; for others to collect, arrange, publish...).

He is still out there: as much for his travels as for his illuminations. To his first publisher, to Jacqueline Arnaud, to Jean-Marie Serreau to make the theater compel and surround him: he's in a rush, as soon his verses, his play's dialogues, his novel's chapters have been handed over, he wants to be out there. The elsewhere calls, and that is how he traveled across the open spaces of Algeria, France, the world, like a hurried passenger, sometimes painfully vulnerable, and shy, and irascible!

Some of the melancholy and gentle bitterness of the older Si Mohand—who chose to wander until he breathed his last breath, spending only two final months in a hospital in Michelet before dyingæsome of the quatrains, even in translation, anticipate the later Yacine in the brilliance of his *Oeuvre en fragments* [Work in Fragments].

The first time I met Yacine was in the summer of '58 in Tunis, when we were there as refugees: he was shy and silent, but inseparable from Harikès, his guitarist friend, and it was the guitar that, upon a sign from him, would speak in his place.

During that time, a group of us would always come together in the same way: commentaries on the war, news from "inside" via this or that resistance worker who had recently arrived, and already we would be looking around to check if "Boussouf's men" weren't lurking about, zealous informers. Not a word about literature, not a line of verse happily fired off: only the nasal moan or the traditional rhythm of a lament from Harikès' guitar. In fact, at the age I was then (though I had published my first two novels) he was without a doubt the first Algerian poet, traditional or "modern," with whom I came in contact in the flesh!

The last time I saw him was on the occasion of a colloquium in Brussels in November '88. The first evening was planned to honor the Brussels production, thirty years earlier, of Kateb's Le Cadavre encerclé *[The Encircled Corpse], after the play was banned in France. With his widow and children present, it was above all an homage to Jean–Marie Serreau who had died. Kateb was among those seated on the stage looking rather glum—he had announced that he wouldn't speak about the Algerian situation with any journalists there!*

I was sitting in the audience, where I quickly became fascinated by Kateb's feet. He was wearing jeans, I think; basically, he stretched his legs and suddenly his feet in rather bulky sneakers took up the whole area at the front of the stage. He had been grumbling earlier; he had repeated that he had nothing to say. For me, his feet, exposed this way in heavy sneakers—and just above them his sad face appearing emaciated and unsmiling—were speaking for him! Or rather, they spoke his silence! The others began to discuss Le Cadavre encerclé, *so that just two actors could have stood up and thrust the fire of the text at us again!*

I grew uncomfortable. I left discreetly. Standing at the bar with a cup of coffee, I was joined by Nabile Farès. I tried to explain my embarrassment to him: like a knot inside me against this kind of commemoration, perhaps also against all commemorations.

"Nabile," I said suddenly, "It isn't Kateb who's dead! It's Jean-Marie Serreau who's gone!... But Kateb, he's still alive! He's not even sixty: he has at least ten more years to write and publish, perhaps fifteen!"

Farès responded that this was the rule in such ceremonies! I answered that because of Kateb's silence, I had been under the impression that he, though still living, was being embalmed!

That evening, accompanied by his German son whom he had found again, surrounded by a few admiring women, Kateb came to our table to say hello, then left.

I never saw him again.

Before the October disaster with its six hundred dead, in March '88, in a little Parisian restaurant, Kateb Yacine declared out of the blue to Thomas Gennari, the theater director, with whom he was working on a play about Robespierre:

"There is here a force of evil. I feel it upon me!... It is taking a long time to finish.... Death, like the shadow of my shadow, comes to meet me. It will get me in the end, or I will be the one to get it!..."

The leukemia which showed its face in the spring of '89, at the very moment when Mammeri had just been carried off by a car accident, never gave him a moment of peace all summer. He was cared for at the hospital in Grenoble where he died on October 28th, '89. He had just reached sixty.

While Ali Zaamoum, his closest friend, gave up on the solemn rituals of the funeral, to think of him in his mind's eye alone in his village, the poet's body was unloaded at the airport, and, after a whole series of speeches, taken to the tiny place in Ben Aknoun that he used as a *pied-à-terre*.

The group of actors from Sidi Bel Abbes and all the other friends of the poet from Algiers, decided to transform this funeral wake into party, a happening. People cried, people laughed, ranted, spoke to the still body, which of course, all were quite certain, was listening to them.

The following day was the funeral for which a good part of the town was getting ready, just like the personalities representing official culture who had to make themselves seen now that the independent press was covering all the events.

Those who had taken part in the wake over Kateb until dawn were the first to leave in the autumn sunlight, as though going to a fair.

The coffin was loaded into a van which set off. A noisy cortege of vehicles followed. Halfway, the van broke down. To ironic comments from Kateb's friends:

"So, just like Kateb. Another one of his tricks! He'll keep us guessing right up to the end!"

In the street—still in El-Biar—young people, hearing that it was the coffin of the great poet, offered to help: they insisted, it was an honor for them. The crowd packed in. The kids changed the tire, checked the oil in the motor. In their enthusiasm, some of them— four in fact—decided to follow the cortege to see the funeral.

Some of the actors, still slightly drunk, assured them that with Kateb's agreement (claiming they'd spoken with him that very night), they were going to have a party at the cemetery! And everyone fell back into a festive mood.

The funeral carriage arrived at the El-Alia cemetery where the group of officials, of ministerial rank, had already arrived. On the other side, opposite, came en masse a whole series of contingents, mainly young people: several Berber associations, carrying banners with a portrait of the poet and inscriptions in the Tifinagh alphabet, were making their way forward in a muffled din.

Some pointed out that they were getting out of special buses coming from Tizi-Ouzou, to thank the dead poet for his constant and tireless support, a man who never even spoke a word of the Berber tongue.

There were almost more girls and women than men—some of the women ordinary, simple women, heads turbaned with colored scarves. Noise and tumult, heavy footsteps from behind, helped to quiet the group of actors who were approaching as though to a show. They stopped in the wings, suddenly wary and suspicious: this time they weren't going to have the act in the airport played on them...

Journalists and a few photographers came to life, with no order and no discretion. One of them showed concern for the family. Someone pointed out, quite close by, Kateb's youngest son, a fifteen-year old, Amazigh, whose gaze was wandering through the crowd: he doesn't understand, he is faraway from the damp open grave, and doesn't know that these are the last moments, that he will never again contemplate the shrouded body of his father as he did last night, amidst lyrical chants, recitals of poems, that— A photographer machine-guns him with his camera flash: two women nearby step in, in an effort to protect him from this.

Suddenly the sun breaks out, as though it were not autumn, as though dawn were about to become fixed in its flickering. Oblique rays light up part of the crowd: stirring up the waiting excavation.

Men, children climb onto the high points, trample on the other tombs: to be there at the crucial moment.

The disorder dies down. Whispers are heard: "The imam, the imam," as a quite venerable personage comes up to take his place in the front row, next to the official group.

Everyone wants to see the precise moment of interment. But, after a moment's hesitation (the imam has placed himself, as though on stage, hands together, palms open, ready in his role as religious officiant), undoubtedly because, through the ranks of the crowd, the word had raced: "The imam, the imam ... for the prayer." Immediately the chants became more feverish: the hymns, sweeping from the depths of the cemetery towards the grave, meet and pass, mingle: in Berber, in dialectal Arabic, in French.

After a pitching and rolling gap, a moment of suspense, there bursts out then, stronger and more full-throated than the others, the *Internationale.* The lines stream in, not quite certain of themselves, it's the first time in a Muslim cemetery. In the refrain many voices join in, and the song fills the space: some of the students are overjoyed, one raising his arm, another brandishing Yacine's photograph.

"I thought for a second the miracle had occurred: Kateb was hearing this song, his song! At the moment where the body raised by four of his friends was about to sink into the earth, I'm quite sure of it, he quivered a last time, thanks to that song! He was happy!" remembers one of the young bystanders.

On the other side patriotic songs broke out again, bringing a halt to the *Internationale.* The officials became rigid with fear, as though the crowd were about to let loose... against them. Quick, the moment for the prayer for the absent. They'll be able to go...

The farewell ceremony carries on. The imam has been trying, at the first lull in the songs and chants, to start his speech, but he is forestalled by a friend of the poet in the name of *Alger républicain*. He speaks, in Arab dialect and in French, of Yacine's young days with the newspaper, then of their personal friendship throughout the years of yesterday's war.

The Communist friend has been talking a little more than five minutes: the audience has become silent and attentive. Immediately afterwards the imam takes steps forward and begins... in classical Arabic.

Roars of rage: violent words hurled against false majesty: "Treason!" shouts one student. The Berber chants rise up from everywhere, this time to drown out the speech. From the background the first "youyous" of the women bore into, pierce the uproar. And still the oblique rays of the sun throw a halo around the picture. The edges of the grave no longer seem black, rather gray, or a subdued blue. Amazigh, the son of the deceased, keeps his eyes glued to these colors.

The imam has stopped speaking: his face calm, he now stares out at the front rows of the crowd: over there the block of actors, there the students from the various associations, here the women, teachers with their pupils. He quickly notices its heterogeneity: worthies (venerable old militants wanting to show for a last time their high regard for the poet: with taut faces, they are shocked that the burial is not taking place with either the serenity or the gravity necessary.... Then the ministers, the officials on duty, who seem ill at ease).

The imam looks at the open grave in which the body has been placed: he focuses on the dead man. "A creature of God, at this moment, that is all!" He begins silent prayers for the dead man. He keeps his ears pricked: the hubbub will die down, he thinks.

Does he then think: "The hubbub of the infidels," "the unaware, the children?" His gaze, firm and strong, remains fixed on the depths of the grave which is catching the rays of the morning sunlight.

The officials start to feel reassured: they sense the determination of the master of ceremonies. "The poet, quick, bury the poet: bury his word. At last!" The imam will tame the crowd: and they will be able to go off, the Minister of Cults, the Minister of Culture, the Minister of Information, the Minister...

Hardly have the mingled clamors and imprecations died down than the imam comes forward, once more with resolution, to issue his first sentence, in a dialect both vigorous and clear:

"O friends of the deceased, whom God has in his safekeeping, I beg you, I beg you my brothers, let us, let us all together allow Kateb Yacine to take his rest."

Attention becomes focused upon the speech which now plays only on the chord of friendship and simple humanity. This writer "this great writer," he says to be more precise, "has struggled all his life: Let us allow him, for the first time, to take his rest," he repeats.

A group of women in scarves is suddenly taken by emotion: one bursts into sobs. The young people become silent: so, Yacine is really dead. What is the point of making him yet again the subject of confrontation?

The imam spoke, in the same tone, two or three sentences, then, aware of the respite he had gained, he began, in a different voice, one with a nasal twang, like that of a tenor in a concert, to read the Koranic liturgy.

Towards the end of the sacred text—delivered more and more rapidly, with the worthies not daring to take up in echo the verses—some of the young people again pierced the renewed silence with two or three enraged slogans: "Long live Berber culture!" "Long live free Algeria!" was taken up by someone else. The names Kateb and Yacine were again hurled into the air by clear women's voices, and their "youyous" a last time burst forth, like the last rockets of a fireworks show.

The sun, still splendid, continued to blind the groups leaving with regret. Around the grave of Kateb, now filled, they had, in the following days, to repair the damage to the surrounding sepulchers.

These were the last funeral rites of an Algeria which was certainly in tumult, but had not yet lurched over into the bottomless pit of war resuscitated.

In 1990, as I returned by train from Lille where I had delivered an address to some students, I decided to stop off in Arras for Robespierre.

The preceding month, they had wanted to dedicate his statue in the city of his birth, but this had unleashed a riot. They resigned themselves to having it in the interior of the courthouse where he had begun his career as a lawyer.

But I had stopped here also for Kateb who had written a play about Robespierre: it had been performed just once, at the municipal theater, the week before. Surely I would find a poster or some other information. (Since Kateb's death, they had been looking for the text of this work, to no avail.)

And so I stepped off the train late in the morning one spring day, I think it was. Nothing at the municipal theater: not a trace of the performance. As I insisted at the ticket window, nothing; not even a response. "Le Bourgeois sans–culotte," was that the title of the play? No, they didn't know it. Kateb Yacine? That meant nothing to the employees at the theater of Arras. Robespierre, yes of course, and the faces closed down.

I walked deliberately through this vast city with its four-sided and majestic squares, with its almost early century atmosphere. My mind was besieged by Kateb's last effort, which had pushed him to follow in the footsteps of the great revolutionary; why was there no text all of a sudden, why this voracious forgetfulness of such a recent performance?

I stopped for a moment inside the courthouse, in front of the bust of the Incorruptible One; a hero all but disavowed, hated even here in his own city. The silence of the place...

And Kateb today, in Algeria? Certainly, after his funeral, they stated and restated to what extent the imams of the fundamentalist mosques had made him into a target of fiery speeches: he deserved every insult, every *fatwa*, while on the other side he was surely laughing out loud.

These new prosecutors had never read a single line by Kateb; of course, they must have been told about the singing of the *Internationale* amidst the muslim graves. A Muslim Brother, a chief who had been brought from Egypt to play the role of philosophic master, even on national television, actually decreed that the play, *Mohammed, prends ta valise* [*Mohammed, Pack Your Bags*], which Kateb had written about the plight of the emigrant from the Maghreb in Europe, was blasphemous...against the prophet Mohammed.

Emboldened by his influence, he had publicly preached against the fact that the remains of such a disbeliever had been brought back home rather than having been left to be buried in Christian soil!

In November '89 all this still had the makings of a farce! Two, three years later, Algeria was deeply immersed in tragedy.

And I think of the Cry of Robespierre, the day his life ended when they took the bandage off his broken jaw. One cry, then a long silence that carried him all the way to the scaffold.

As he tried to finish this final play, Kateb had wanted to give it the title, "The Cry of Robespierre." A cry, then silence at the hour of death.

Hereafter it is the silence of our purest writer. From October '88, one year before his death.

FOUR WOMEN AND ONE FAREWELL

I

Anna Gréki, born Colette Grégoire in 1931, spent the first four years of her life in the Aurès in Ménaâ. She was the daughter of a *pied-noir* schoolteacher, who was *laïc* [nonreligious] and socialist. After studying in Collo and then in Philippeville, she still could not forget that early paradise.

> *Everything I love and all that I do now*
> *Have their roots there*
> *Beyond the Pass of Guerza in Ménaâ*
> *Where my first friend, I know, will wait for me.*

Twenty-seven years later, imprisoned at Barberousse in Algiers as a Communist militant and supporter of the Nationalist cause, she writes one poem after another:

> *My childhood and the delights*
> *In Ménaâ—the diverse community of Arris...*
> *Now, too, war is in my village!*

After her arrest, she had been tortured. She withstood it; she "held out," and was forever marked by it, she who was so refined; her luminous face with the auburn hair and the green eyes, her tiny body, her whole strong and fragile person would retain a kind of haze from this, a silent and never spoken suffering—for the nine years of life that remained.

During this time she will write; she will marry Jean, a friend, also from here, who will help her when she comes out of prison, when they are expelled together to France, and in Tunis they will join the leadership of the Algerian struggle again.

She will be marked just as much by her first great love, from before the Algerian War: a young student from Tlemcen, Ahmed Inal. He joined the Resistance when she was arrested. She cannot forget him; in her cell she speaks to him:

Before your awakening.
I understood nothing of what they said to me
And I was calling wisdom a stubborn desert
My only desires were to bemoan them...

She spends a year at Barberousse; in November '58, they transfer her to the camp of Beni-Messous. Is it only then that she learns of the death of young Inal: while fighting in the Resistance. Nothing is less certain... Perhaps, sadly, a victim of "purges" by this or that warrior leader against young recruits whose faith seemed as much Communist as Nationalist.

Anna Gréki—whose name is still Colette—hears of the suspicious circumstances surrounding her loss—just as she, expelled at the same time as Jean, is finally able to taste her newfound, desperately desired freedom.

The death of her great love. And this silent friend close to her struggle who loves her in silence. They marry and arrive in Tunis early in 1959.

The young couple tries to relearn how to live in this small community of Algerian refugees; they want to make themselves useful, build for tomorrow... Jean protects his wife: he is acutely aware that on certain evenings the memory of her beloved resistance fighter will return (*"Where did he die? How did they kill him? Is it really possible? His own brothers?... Here in Tunis they say... for Abane Ramdane!..."*), but she wants to forget the darkness; she wants to believe...in the Revolution!

She is pregnant, happily so. She and Jean with their young boy will be among the first to go home to the independent Algeria.

Her first collection of poetry, *Algérie, capitale Alger* [*Algeria, Algiers*], is published by Jean Oswald. The strength of her first poems alongside the fragility of her memories of the Aurès. Already, Algerian students are learning them by heart, chanting:

I no longer know how to love other than with fury in my heart!

Encouraged, Anna begins to write all the time. Jean and she find an apartment: disorder, expansion, and sometimes the almost crazy gaiety of friends found again, lost and found again.... The dead are there, too, as if seated in the sky of Algiers, contemplating the people from the countryside who, whole families together, have come to settle in a jumble in many of the European neighborhoods.

Sometimes Anna thinks she sees—a hallucination?—young Inal standing in the sun. No, she won't go back to Tlemcen.

The two brothers of the dead man have come back to the eastern part of the country. Anna sits down across from them, opposite their wives (one, a Berber, formerly detained, who admires Anna's poems; the other, a gracious Ecuadorian). Anna listens to the two brothers and, in spite of herself, looks for a resemblance, an echo.... She is expressionless; that night, she nestles up to Jean. She takes care of her boy. She decides to begin classes at the university again and to finish her degree.

She writes; always poems. Thus she immerses herself in her childhood again, then in her first love.

Her anxiety resurfaces, most likely in 1965. Yet, she finds a teaching job in the former Bugeaud secondary school. She goes there on foot. She has crowded classes: all adolescents, girls and boys together. She introduces them to French poetry, to the riches of the language. She is entirely devoted.

One time, she dares. She writes a line of verse on the board: it had besieged her head and eyes during her morning walk.

"Do you like it?" she asks.

"Oh yes!" a girl eagerly stamps her feet.

Another one rises and solemnly recites the beginning of the poem, then shyly:

"Madame, look, I counted! It's an alexandrine!"

"Do you want the rest of the poem?" Anna asks, with a hopeful heart.

There is a solid yes. And so it happens that the rhythms inside her come sliding off her tongue enthusiastically in the middle of her classes.

Then she goes home in a furrow of silence, which she plows right through the dense, sometimes half-rural crowd. Anna pays attention only to the hum, to the sky down there above the harbor. Without a doubt, thanks to the school and especially to the young girls and their so discreet and admiring complicity, Anna tells herself that the shadows

of the past will surely vanish, despite Jean's worries at work (his growing responsibilities in the economic sector are stirring up jealousy).

Then comes Ben Bella's fall from power in 1965. The military
arrives: Communists and Anarchists are arrested. What might remain
of the good days is auctioned off. Some flee; others leave. Algiers is
emptied of its utopia that admittedly was coming to an end all by itself.

Anna hears that some people close to her have been arrested; one of
the poets she loves, they say, has been tortured horribly before being
sent to the South: and so the filthy beast returns, the tortured of yesterday are the torturers today, others.... How does it happen? On a
nightmarish stage, the place still hot, the irons still blazing red, those
at work there simply inverting their masks!...

At the end of this alley or there, behind that façade, hidden by
that wall, yes, the dirty deed had lingered, lying in wait, the place still
hot! Yesterday's cries will start up again, or rather no, they continue.
*"If I hear just once that a girl, a woman has thus been handed over to
"them," if...I shall kill myself, ah yes, in this city I shall throw myself, I
shall drown myself in the Mediterranean! If..."*

But they have forgotten about Anna. At school she is a fine
teacher. Her husband, Jean, has never been registered in the Communist Party.

Anna writes; with her students at school she is the same: except
that she no longer writes the poems that come to her on the board.

Like a naked bird and the color jumps
At my throat anger ocean color
Blood anger turned the color of high tide
Like a whip lashing the eyes black anger
Cuts off my breath, cuts off my

Arms and legs. Knives of fire. Stones cast
At my body. Anger beats upon my wounds.

In the summer of '65, Anna regularly phones an Algerian friend who has left to live in Paris. Alice is a psychiatrist. Anna's voice asks her more and more repeatedly for a tranquilizer, an anti-depressant.

They speak gently with each other. Alice is concerned.

One day, Anna tells her on the phone that she is pregnant: four months already. She has decided to stop teaching sooner. There are no further calls from Algiers to Paris.

On the 5th of January 1966, Anna Gréki goes to the maternity clinic with Jean: they have to help her save the child who at seven months is premature. They have to...

Anna has lost so much weight: a transfusion is considered necessary. During the night, for lack of sufficient supplies, despite the care that came too late, Anna dies. An accident...

Anna is dead, Alice hears of it in Paris.

Busy with the funeral arrangements, Jean compiles the last manuscript of poems (it will be published); he also discovers an unfinished novel.

"An accident?" he keeps repeating in Algiers, where he will not leave with his boy for several more years.

Anna Gréki was to be buried one sunny day.

   That morning the sun
   Had the voice of a public crier
Anna's poetic work, vibrant with fervor and strength—she, so vulnerable—has been translated into Arabic.

<u>2</u>

Taos: in the end, she came to this name rather late, or came back to it—the name of the female peafowl, which characterizes her more than any other.

Born of Kabylian parents who converted to Christianity, the only daughter among five boys, and born as an emigrant—in 1913 in Tunis—what could have been more natural than to provide her with two first names (like her brothers, born in the mountain village: they have a Muslim first name given by the Amrouche grandparents and a Christian first name given by the white priests who baptize them).

The little girl, running around the streets in the Italian quarter of Tunis, is named Marie-Louise. Her father, stubbornly wearing his original fez, goes to Sunday mass to sing Gregorian chants; but at home, her mother Fadhma-Marguerite, who dresses like her neighbors, Sicilian women, feels she is first of all Berber, despite her weakness for French poets (Lamartine, Hugo), that she had studied at the French school, down there, back home in Kabylia...

She has an unspoken rivalry with her mother-in-law—Belkacem had her come—for the father in the village has two wives, sometimes three, depending on his constitution. The grandmother, a pious Muslim, goes to the medina and frequents the great mosque and the many sanctuaries; she speaks Berber with the family.

The grandmother persists in calling the little girl, named Marie-Louise, Taos, the name of the peacock, and that is how Taos is immersed from the beginning in a bath of languages: the street languages, Italian and Sicilian, the colloquial Arabic of Tunis, the language at school, French of course, which she reads and writes, and finally the language of exile and of the family secret, the Berber of Kabylia. Every evening, the grandmother and her son have long talks in Berber—the language of cries and conflict (Belkacem with his older sons), and of the drama of daily life. It is especially the language in which Fadhma hereafter will sing of her nostalgia and the wounds of her maternal heart!

Marie-Louise listens; takes time to really listen: this is truly her source, obscure and all–consuming. She will go as far as Bône/Hippone (another double name) and, remembering the haunting chant of her mother's voice, she will start to become, she will become the regal Taos Amrouche.

From 1936 to 1962 runs the long road of the young girl, the woman, the nomad, the enthusiast who settles in Paris in 1945. Novelist, radio producer, ethnologist of her ancestral folklore, she leads a multi–faceted active life: she always lives passionately and fully.

She sings her maternal repertoire, but until the sixties she only rarely appears in public.

It is without a doubt her brother's death—Jean, whom she loved devotedly, who remained the hero of her adolescence, whom she carried as a part, the most valiant part of herself from the moment he was gone—it is this death, then, that set her free while it made her grow. Freed her first from her rages, from her narcissism, from her woman's passions and suffering.

She is going to be fifty years old: her body is getting to know the first assaults of her illness. Fifteen years. She will struggle for fifteen years with the cancer that will get the better of her; for now her voice is intact, it comes to her from the great depths of the centuries of the language, her voice with its invincible strength...

On this 2nd day of April '62, she sang for Jean Amrouche who has closed his eyes forever—it was the "Song of Joy."

The stages of slow and sure ascension of the great priestess Taos Amrouche lie inscribed into the years from 1962 to 1976. She stands erect, she rants; sometimes she wraps her very fierce language in vocalizations—inspired by Spanish flamenco—reinfusing its authentic harshness and an inconsolable melancholy.

She is there, on every stage in Europe, in concert halls—the greatest ones—and in some churches or monasteries, almost an officiating priestess. She sings a cappella and still she populates the stage with her invisible tribe, bards, shepherds, women of all ranks, smart, fickle and outcast. She sings the songs of Muslim pilgrims who, during the last century, would visit Cheikh Mohand, or Lhocine, she interprets them with spirit and gravity, she who was born of Christian converts.

For she sings of her heritage above all; she carries all the deeprootedness within her, through her small body draped in the immaculate toga, her face wreathed in ancient jewelry, in her magnificent and proud voice she recalls the past: what weighs heavily and cannot be denied, what binds and transfigures you, what propels you way up high, to heaven!

The singer's faith dazzled so many great names in poetry, music, letters, and the arts, from Olivier Messiaen to André Breton, who salutes "the song of the phoenix" in her: Algeria then was bent beneath the yoke or screaming from the injuries of war. Taos was there to remind us of ancestral invincibility, the wholly disinterested pride that certain people find unbearable...

In her novels—from *Jacinthe noire*, written before '40, published in '47 by Charlot in Paris and for some obscure reason never distributed, to *L'Amant imaginaire*, with *La Rue des tambourins* in between—so moving for its Tunisian and Kabylian childhood memories—more often than not, Taos plowed the writer's furrow in bitter solitude. It was the stage where she was consecrated as a masterful interpreter of the words of the Ancestors.

I am coming to the circumstances of her death, Taos then more than ever the peacock—haughty and totally erect, almost joyful in the face of adversity.

There was her first concert in Fez in 1939. There was her last one in Amiens in January 1976, three months before her death.

For each of these, the singer posed for a photographer: at her point of departure and at the last stop on her warrior's itinerary.

In '39, in Fez: so very young, she had traveled there by train from Tunis—having been encouraged by Gabriel Audisio as well as by Philippe Soupault, the Surrealist poet who directed Radio-Tunis.

She stood, lovely debutante, in front of an audience of Moroccan notables, connoisseurs of traditional music, and the director of the Casa Vélasquez who had retired here.

On stage her ample voice miraculously fans out to the rear of the concert hall, Berber cavalrymen from the Middle Atlas accompany her and, in the end, start the first ripple of applause going.... She appears like a warrior, an Antinea rising from the sands: a young girl of twenty-six, yet so frail, photographically preserved in her long dress of white satin, with an almost sophisticated elegance, this child of poor Kabylian emigrants.

At the end of this first success, a tall and plain Frenchman, looking severe and accompanied by his wife, comes to bow to her: he is a connoisseur of many forms of Berber music. He introduces himself: "Doctor Secret!" he mumbles before disappearing.

Thirty-seven years later, it is her last concert—although her illness had tormented her for weeks, Taos had wanted, with the help of her daughter, to make it to Amiens, to stand tall, inhabited by the same untouched voice, to reveal the hymns, the melodies, and laments before the enthusiastic audience.

Her previous concert had taken place more than six months earlier, the last in a series of performances given in Paris at the Théâtre du Châtelet. After she had sung for a long time, as always, a cappella, she spoke, her voice resonating like a vibrant testament, eliciting from the audience women's ululations and wave upon wave of collective emotion:

"As long as I have one breath of life left in me, I wish that this breath of life be put into service on behalf of these songs, which are the glory and the treasure of humanity!"

This evening, at the Maison de la Culture of Amiens, while they watch her from the wings, afraid that she may collapse, she continues to stand as straight as ever, exhausted but smiling, and waits through the audience's many curtain calls.

The curtain falls. Her daughter and her friends take her back to her dressing room. She has barely caught her breath when an old man, tall and severe, dressed in black, appears before her:

"Do you remember your first concert in Fez, Madame? In 1939. I was a doctor in that city. I came to congratulate you; I was accompanied by my wife who is now dead.... My name is Doctor Secret," he ended gently before leaving.

Taos remembered, his name and the couple. She smiles, thanks him, is moved. The old man leaves.

She then turns to her daughter, Laurence; looking sad, she draws a closed circle in the air with her finger:

"At the first and at the last concert!" she sighs. "It really is over; this man is the messenger!"

She asks to be taken home as quickly as possible to Paris, to the Batignolles. She goes to bed, knowing that this time she will not rise to sing again.

The last photograph, taken on her sickbed at her request, shows her even more full of pathos.

In recent months, she has had real success in the bookstores with her novel *L'Amant imaginaire.* She has sung so much these last years; she sings in her head, she hums at dawn to forget the medical treatment with its outrages and hardships.

She is preparing herself.

She is preparing herself for departure. As she did once before for Jean, her brother; as eight years ago for her old mother, for Fadhma, who left her *Histoire de ma vie,* such a rare bequest, to the women of the Maghreb.

Jean died in Paris; Fadhma in Brittany. Only her father, Belkacem, is buried in the village, in Ighil-Ali. Taos kneeled on his grave only a few years earlier.

She is preparing herself; soothing herself.

One morning she asks for a hairdresser. In front of her astonished family, she gives the order...for him to shave her head.

"Let them photograph me this way!" she adds bravely.

And she smiles for her photographer friend: she shows her family, she shows us all her mask of a woman in her sixties—her gaze stares at us from so far off, and her smile neither frozen nor constrained, with that undefinable expression of hers, getting ready to depart.

She, Taos, the exiled one, the rooted one, has completed her task.

She faces death and, since there will be no more celebrations or concerts, it is this encounter that the photograph must eternalize as the message, she decides.

Taos Amrouche died a few days later on the 2nd of April, 1976, in Paris. She was buried, as she wished to be, in Provence, close to her flower-filled home in Saint-Rémy: neither too far nor too close to the land of her Ancestors.

3

Josie and her big gypsy eyes.... And above all her voice, that happy contralto. For she would laugh—she loved to laugh!... How will I ever learn to grow old, now that Josie Fanon, my elder, cannot show me the way with her laughter and her brazen humor?

And my daughter—during the years she was a student in Algiers, Josie was a second mother to her—as soon as my daughter heard the news in Paris (it was the voice of the author of *Déserteur* on the phone with me one morning) she took the plane. Was there at the funeral.

Stayed two or three days in Algiers; with Olivier, now an orphan, and a young adolescent boy, Karim, the neighbor's son, whom Josie had taken care of since he was a child.

My daughter then returned to Paris. Was silent for a long time. And then finally told me, one evening, about Josie's last weeks and days.

In June, she had made the trip to the Tunisian border to visit Frantz's grave. (I am sure that it was then she made her decision: to join him.)

In Tunis, she returned to every place they had lived. Back in El-Biar, she took several days to put all her things in order: photographs, poems she was writing, Frantz's letters which she had compiled and arranged much earlier, letters of her son, her friends.

She gave her young neighbor, Karim, various presents, "to remember me by" she told him gently when he'd protest or try to refuse, his heart fearful.

She made sure the cleaning woman was even more meticulous. She would linger, I feel it, every morning to listen to the sounds of neighboring families rising from the courtyard: I see her low bedroom, filled with multi-colored rugs where we would stay, the window open as if above a well, to catch the rising noises, women's laughter, whining children.

I hear Josie letting herself be wrapped in these sounds of Algerian life, by this everyday profusion.

But she has decided: since her visit to Frantz's grave; she is determined.

She phones her son in Paris to reassure him: yes, she will start therapy again with the family psychologist. Yes, he wants to hospitalize her for a week or two, no more. Her son should put his mind at rest, she will do it. No, she does not feel alone: he should not be worried; there's no need whatsoever for him to come.

And so she willingly went to the hospital. On the condition, she told the doctor, that they let her go home to her apartment on the weekend: be with her flowers, the sounds of the neighbors, the concern of Karim and his mother.

She rested in the hospital for six days. She brought books, music. She read; even more she daydreamed, looking at the summer light from her bed. Hardly spoke.

"She was smiling at us when she left," a nurse recalled, unable to forget the gentleness in Josie's large eyes, her voice so near.

Josie went home to El-Biar on Thursday evening.

"I'll be there Friday!" she declared.

The nurse waited for her on Saturday. Very early on the previous day, by the light of dawn, Josie opened the window of her living room that looked out onto the street. Pulled a chair over. Took off her shoes. In one or two seconds, glanced around the rooms in which everything was in its place. A last glance at the geraniums on the neighboring balcony.

With her back finally turned on her home and her life, Josie Fanon threw herself out of her fifth–story window.

The 13th of July, 1989; El-Biar, above Algiers. A Friday.

In her fall, Josie hurt no one: only she exploded.

I think of these three women's destinies over the course of a little more than twenty years in independent Algeria!

As for me, I had returned to my country on the first day of freedom, I was working as an academic but left on an impulse three years later: they wanted to establish an authorization procedure "to leave the territory," and thus I would depend on bureaucrats for my movements and my travels!...I went back to Paris, the city where I'd spent my twenties!...I returned home again in '74 to work conducting sociological surveys under the direction of M'Hamed Boukhobza, seeking through cinema to invent both a reality and a dream at once; during those explorations I profited from the advice, or sometimes just the companionship, of Abdelkader Alloula. I left again in '79 or '80.

Thereafter, I settled into a constant coming-and-going, resigned myself to this between-two-worlds, between-two-lives, between-two-freedoms, one of deeply diving backward, the other of rushing forward and, each time, glimpsing a new horizon!...

These three women come and go as well, between Algeria and France; haunted by what, by yesterday's war, by our tenacious ancestors, by the tribe's voice for Taos, by the loves of her Berber childhood for Anna.... They come and go in their own way, these three women who write until their final farewell!

A farewell I receive shortly afterwards, or a long time later, now in the crater of this account of the dead, of their procession which I arrange while hoping against hope that one of them would have escaped.

I have assembled these three silhouettes today because I miss these women: alas, what a women's literature we would have brought into the world, from the braziers filled with embers and ashes, and the patios packed with whining children!...

Writing that would not only have been about flight, like the passage of the stork parting but who, at the last moment, from high up on the towers, stays long enough to watch the small courtyards stirring with so many young and adolescent girls—the song in honor of the stork has become a recurrent theme of female folklore.

Writing for the ages or, at the very least, a literature of comings and goings, to remember our grandmothers by, our grandmothers who made up stories, who invented, without writing.

Leaning back against this white, this slow obliteration, filling one's whole soul with it before confronting it head on.

Not a farewell, my friends. Not yet!

<u>4</u>

Over fifteen years ago at the University of Algiers, I was aware that one of my female students had become a devoted practicing Muslim.

Principal of a middle school in the outskirts of Algiers, she would go to work with her hair covered by a white, embroidered *tchador.* Having also raised two children who were now students themselves, she seemed to have found, in her work and her choice of life, an intrinsic harmony with the country in transformation. Certainly, I said to myself, her father's origin—a German convert to Islam, who had long ago immigrated to this northern town, who married and raised his family there—could have made her especially vulnerable for a time, when she was very young! "Do I really belong to this land, this country in search of itself?" she must have wondered at times.

I remember her beautiful face, her bright eyes; I even remember the work she would hand in to me, especially on theater.

I have tried to imagine, fifteen years later, her face, her gaze wreathed in the white satin of her headdress, similar after all to the traditional urban women of my childhood, though they were kept sequestered.

It was she, undoubtedly comforted by her teaching life, where every day she was guiding the destiny of young people searching for knowledge, a profession, a future...It was she whom they warned in her office one October day in 1994:

"Madame, two policemen are with the concierge asking to see you!"

She showed no surprise on the phone.

"Have them come upstairs!"

Right afterwards, she turned to her secretary; her face had suddenly gone pale, she murmured:

"Leave the room, but stay next door: they're coming for me, I know it!"

The secretary automatically obeyed, a little later recognizing the note of anxiety, or rather a kind of anguished premonition.

Barely had the discomfitted young girl sat down next door, when, after the noise of the policemen entering the room, the shooting began on the other side of the door: they aimed pointblank at the principal whose hair was covered in white...

"Fake policemen! They're fake policemen!" was shouted in the hallways, while the two executioners, calmly retreating as they kept their guns trained on the terrified crowd, moved towards the exit.

It had been a month since "the madmen of God" had decreed the school strike they wanted to impose upon the population—a distant echo, no doubt, of the "Battle of Algiers" that Abane Ramdane had conceived and then organized during the seven days of the general strike.

To explain the murder of this teacher, however, some people recalled that a year earlier a very wellknown imam, of the same pacifist Islamic movement, had been kidnapped in Blida—the town the principal had come from. He had expressed a stubborn refusal to support any violence in the name of Islam, by any declaration to the faithful.

Obstinate to the point of heroism, the cheikh Bouslimani was certainly tortured and, after a few days during which his moral conscience remained firm, was assassinated.

PROCESSION 3

I

I have often wondered, how the plans are made in this citadel of sunshine, the plans between torturers?

During the months of the "Battle of Algiers" in 1957? The French parachutists, with their imposing appearance, their leather boots, their well-nourished virility, their commands to third parties, the voiceless servants, and the gleaming gray of the metallic instruments, and the clouded atmosphere, the clean design of electric wires, the water on the floor they wade through, mixed with blood and urine, one torture chamber after another... Of course, the easiest thing, to close one's ears, look at it all as if at a painting, shut oneself off from the death rattles, the screams, the harrying raucous voices: a pure spectacle, an ice-blue nightmare!

Before, on the heights of Algiers, in El-Biar, in the Clos-Salembier, in the lovely Moorish villas changed into human laboratories...Suddenly I'm thinking of that romantic madman, the French poet, writer, and philosopher who came to see with his own eyes, I mean Maurice Clavel, who returned from his descent into the Algerian hell with a novel, Djamila, which he gave to me in 1958 on the stairs at my publisher's...

Yes, almost forty years later I wonder whether, here in these palaces of horror, it was at the moment when his torments came to an end that one of the tortured began eagerly to desire being a torturer himself one day? No doubt, the imposing presence of the inquisitor who orders the human dogs around, who parades his omnipotence!

Is that how it happened, when the heart of Algiers was given over to terror, at risk of yielding to the obsessive fear of never-ending screaming, was it in this sticky darkness of the city that the new plans were made?

Right after 1982, or perhaps even before: professional policemen, Algerians who saw themselves as patriots, struggling for independence, also learned "special practices" from professionals of brother nations, friendly states...This time, there was no role reversal whatsoever, a simple transfer of technical assistance. Commonplace practices for an all too common future State.

Bachir Hadj Ali, a poet, musicologist, and for a long time the secretary of the Algerian Communist Party, suffered repeated and ghastly tortures after he was arrested in September 1965.

Thus the hideous practice reappears, in good conscience, without the pretext of blunders, for reasons of state almost. Violent interrogations, condemned as soon as the day after independence, continued on the sly, practiced and, it was rumored, by overzealous professionals well–trained on the outside! Already.

But the tortures which Hadj Ali describes in detail in *L'Arbitraire* (published by Editions de Minuit in 1966, the Algerian edition not until 1991), this report of renewed torture follows in the wake of *La Question* in 1958 by Henri Alleg. (Except that at that time the independent press did not exist in Algeria; the intellectuals who could have raised this topic in diatribes and public debate had either been exiled or reduced to silence!)

L'Arbitraire describes in detail, and almost with a glint in his eye (the very special gaiety of Bachir, child of the Casbah), several of the torturers' faces to whom he gives masks that have greater significance than their identities. There's "the Wild Boar, a pinhead on a very brown block of flesh and grease"; "el-Halouf, the fake tough guy, disgusting and pitiful"; there's also "Beelzebub, the monkey of Mouzaïa, always hiding behind his dark glasses and nervously hopping around during torture sessions"; there's "the Thug, a wild cat" who would be "enraged" by his victim's silence; and finally, "at the head of this factory, the Red-head, a Socialist torturer, concerned about the unity of revolutionary activists when they leave their tormentors' bathtub!"

Bachir's accusatory testimony gradually turns into a lyrical text, love poems written when leaving this hell—suffered in several locations in Algiers (sometimes even the same ones as in 1957).

After two weeks on a hunger strike and before being transferred to Lambèse, then to Aïn-Sefra, the poet resolutely concludes:

"I glimpsed the weak point in the enemy's system. I infiltrated it, I hugged it close and let it empower my silence.... I conclude my trial with my honor as an activist intact, and the conviction that a cause is lost as soon as it defends itself through torture!"

Then he frees himself to write a celebration of love for Lucette, his wife:

Yesterday
I loved you and the flame consumed wood
I loved you and salt enriched the blood
I loved you and the earth absorbed the rain
I loved you and the palm tree thrust itself to the sky...

Love's intensity managing to swallow up everything, including the world's horror? When Bachir was still imprisoned, the memory of Lucette's face could block out the presence of executioners, his companions' screams ("with brothers screaming in pain, I know they're alive; and hearing them alive makes me stronger!"). The unshakable optimism and valor of this poet who throughout his long trek through hell remains alive: that is to say joyful, that is to say in love, that is to say still celebrating yesterday's struggle (as in his poems for the 11th of December '60).

This boy from the Casbah of Algiers, this dock worker's son who had to leave school at sixteen, and faced the French courts of justice ten years later, where he firmly declared, just before '54:

"Just as the courts of Louis XVI could not resolve the conflict between the aristocracy and the people of France, the courts of today will not resolve this conflict between the oppressors and the oppressed. Nothing will stop Algerians from loving freedom!"

Bachir Hadj Ali, embraced by the popular musicians of his neighborhood, who would fight for independence clandestinely, and it is he who in April '56 will be the one to negotiate with Abane Ramdane before accepting that "*les maquis rouge*" (the red underground) be integrated into the underground of the F.L.N.

This is the man they arrest and torture when Boumediene arrives on the scene: torture because for reasons of state, they are coming down as hard on the extreme left as on the Communists. During the years he is under house arrest in Aïn-Sefra, he writes a letter to his beloved wife every day. Words of love run all through his work, like the sharp, scrupulous listening to the *Chaabi* music practiced by the artisans, and the music itself of wise and ancient Andalusia...

1974: the political respite intervenes. Bachir Hadj Ali is set free and can return to his life in Algiers in broad daylight.

My first question is still the same, open and bitter. (Hadj Ali, whom I met, most often on the beach with his friends and his wife, loved to laugh, joke around, recall a thousand details of his life..."Even when he would describe his torturers or incidents of his life in prison," mumbles Nadjet, one of his close friends, "he'd laugh and laugh! Admittedly, sometimes he couldn't stop laughing...I can still hear him.")

My first question remains unanswered: how, in Algiers, the black city, did the executioners of yesterday join hands with those of today?

The question will be caught up in the undertow and with force: in November and December to be exact, after the October insurrection in Algiers.

Adolescents are killed by the hundreds by the army to restore order, after which the number of young adolescents only grows. How? By taking up the lists of '65, '66, '67.... The memory of executioners works through lists and files and indelible reports.

The first protests of the democratic resistance finally focuses on this: struggle against torture, condemn it loud and clear. *Le Cahier noir d'Octobre [The Black Notebook of October],* which would be published in Algiers, was the third milestone in this literature of condemnation and testimony. *La Question* in '58, *L'Arbitraire* in '66, and finally this *Cahier noir.*

In late '88, early '89, while our only political party is smashed to pieces, while so many intellectuals join the struggle for democracy, the poet Bachir Hadj Ali is unfortunately elsewhere. Alive, but elsewhere.

His most recent collection of poetry, published in 1978, is called *Mémoires clairières [Clearing Memoirs].*

For a year or two already, Bachir's memory has been spotty on a daily basis, with blanks that torment him. Lucette has always been a teacher; as she leaves in the morning, she tells him at what time she'll be back, sometimes they set a time to meet at the house of close friends.

She has hardly left, he has hardly finished working on his texts or on his study of the traditional musicians of the Casbah, when the time set for their meeting has crept forward in his mind. It is three o'clock and his wife is not back, he panics: there must have been an accident. He phones friends, sometimes one or two hospitals. Faced with this new anxiety, Lucette starts to write down her schedule and their meeting times.

No matter. Every day he thinks he's lost his keys, or believes he's been locked in: imprisoned again. He grows impatient, runs outside; in a panic, he loses his way. His sons go to find him. He quiets down; he regains a clear head; he grows calm.

He is not yet sixty. The first doctors he visits with his wife in Algiers, Paris, and Brussels don't detect the early warning signs of Alzheimer's disease. When, among the tortures Bachir suffered thirteen years earlier, Lucette mentions the torment of the "German drum" in particular (endless beating of a can placed around the victim's head), one or two of the clinicians state:

"Those tortures may have aggravated a preexisting condition!"

He receives constant care, notably a treatment to reactivate the circulation in the brain. Bachir continues his political activity: it is 1980. During some of his speeches his voice stops; he blushes, has a fit of anger that he brings under control.... The thread of his thoughts returns; he smiles.

He suffers anew when he notices that, in his musicological work, his hearing no longer catches the very high notes. When he has this checked, it is verified that his hearing loss is irreversible.

"That must be the result of the 'German drum'!" he thinks.

He suddenly understands that his painstaking study of the Chaabi cantor of the Casbah, M'Hamed el-Anka, which he has been working on for a long time, will remain unfinished. One day he notices that his pen hand falters. The writer in him protests. Yet an even more intense torture.

Without a doubt this was when he made Lucette promise that, should his mind grow dim, she will help him end it all! She promises. She will never be able to keep her oath.

The last escape: one day, he leaves the house by himself, goes toward the beach, desperately looking for the sea.... He must surely have reached it, walked in the waves, looked at the sky, perhaps at children laughing in the distance, heard the voices of women he could not see, a sound.... He eventually came back, having forgotten his original intention amid the humble and quiet sounds of life. It took him a while to find his house again, his anxious family searching for him in all directions.

He arrived, smiling, daydreaming.

"The sea, I wanted the sea!" he said gently in the arms of Lucette, who understood.

From then on she arranged a schedule of shifts for those around Bachir, the patient who would not get better again.

Long years in which Bachir can no longer write, then can no longer speak, then is less and less able to move. He grows serene only in Lucette's presence. His sons are there. His comrades in the struggle come to see him regularly. Mohammed Khedda stays for hours showing him his paintings and drawings. Together they listen to music: traditional Algerian music, but Beethoven and Mozart, too.

Bachir is alive, but not here.

On the 4th of May 1991, Khedda the painter succumbs to lung cancer.

The next morning, Lucette bends over the patient's bed and gently repeats to Bachir:

"Don't worry if I'm gone for a little while.... I'm going to your friend's funeral. Your friend!"

Bachir understood; this time he waited for her calmly, without the usual anxiety. But thereafter he refuses all nourishment. He sees Khedda running, flying away ahead of him, there on the horizon. He wants to join him.

Bachir Hadj Ali dies on the 10th of May 1991.

A few days later, Tahar Djaout ends a long piece about Hadj Ali in *Algérie-Actualité* with these words:

"Fortunately, artists do not live through their physical presence alone. Beyond what nature must take back from them they bequeath to us the fruit of the trees they have planted. How else could we imagine an Algeria without Issiakhem, without Mouloud Mammeri, without Kateb Yacine, without Mohammed Khedda and Bachir Hadj Ali?"

Exactly two years later, in May 1993, the creator of this oration would in turn be missed among Algeria's poets and artists. One day in May at dawn, Tahar Djaout would be killed pointblank by bullets.

2

But what adolescent boy, completing his course of madness set free, killed Tahar? What young warrior went to the borders of Pakistan, trembled, prayed, then killed on behalf of his Afghan brothers, and, wreathed in light, playfully and drunkenly gave himself the title "emir"? Started to pay attention to his clothing, his beard, his toga, the way he walked in the streets of his neighborhood to which he returned? Yes, what warrior indeed, in his incompetence, his anger, in the fury of the group astride the once voiceless revolt searching for a face, going off to find shelter in the hills and forests of the Atlas? What new leader, in the despair that was set in motion when he was twenty-five or thirty, finally had the power of commanding men to go forth against the city—the decayed city, vilified, swollen with money, with policemen, with...

Suddenly it was decided, this emir with his equal beside him, his rival very close by, they all agreed:

"Let's kill the Communists here, too, as yesterday we did in Afghanistan! Let's set our men and boys loose against these so-called men of letters who write, who sign things and makes demands, who..."

"Did you say Djaout?"

"A Communist?"

"A Journalist, same thing!"

"A foreign agent, from the West, from France, from..."

"Let him be the first on our new list, then!"

The emir chooses two boys barely out of puberty. They have the gleam in their eyes of those who want to prove themselves to these heroes who went so far away, returned from nowhere.

One of the leaders throws the last article Djaout has written in the garbage can. Why read? He speaks of liberty, that intellectual? And what about faith in Islam, is that not enough for him? He speaks of a secular State? He should have stayed in Moscow, that's where he came from, of course!...

The young men who've been called together wait. They each carry a weapon. The first one says in a detached voice that it will be the first time he will aim at a man! Everybody knows that, during training, he was the best shot. The second one says nothing. He's already had human targets. For him the essential thing is to hit each one.

The emir, carefully groomed, like an actor playing a new role, his hand caressing his fine brown beard, invites them to share his prayer, beneath the oak tree, behind the hill.

He chants a whole sura. He knows his voice is pure. He wants to reward the two emissaries in advance, so that they will then go forth with their weapons, their spirit filled with his tenor voice. Thus, he tells himself, when they turn their back on him and go down into the plain and from there to the capital, his presence will go with them, and neither of them will have a trembling hand...

Which one of the two emissaries will arrive feverish, at daybreak, in the city—their city—where this Djaout, for months now director of the newspaper *Ruptures,* lives?

Dawn of the rupture for the writer who, before going forth, takes a long look at his photograph of Arthur Rimbaud, the only picture pinned above his work table.

Kenza, a little girl of eight, still in bed, hears her father walk down the hall and then slam the door shut. She lies there daydreaming: "I must tell him this very evening! How I can't wait for vacation to come so that we may return to our village in the mountains, run beneath the olive trees!...I must!"

Outside, the dry interminable crackle of machine-gun fire explodes. The little girl is in the hall, running barefoot, opening the door, standing on the threshold, surrounded by the neighbors who come rushing out. Her father's car disappears at top speed at the end of the street. Close by, four men bend over a body on the ground.

"My father!"

The little girl thinks she screams: the two words never come out.

"Tahar!" her mother shouts behind her.

These two killers, these assassins, these murderers, who are they?

Ten days later, in a dark room, they're staring at the funeral scene, filmed by a French television crew and broadcast live. The young men look at the screen: so it really was a poet whom they targeted, who spent a week in a coma and who is being buried today.... A poet? No, a journalist, a Communist, the emir said so. The TV is lying, as usual.

On the screen, Tahar's mother gives voice spontaneously to her grief. In the darkness of the room, one of the men translates the Berber words.

The people there, the faces, the simplicity of the surroundings, the naked sorrow of the women. The one for whom the mother's words are translated mumbles that the emir has perhaps mistaken the name.... The other retorts that the emir knows, cannot make mistakes. Silence in the darkness of the room.

The first one gets up, extinguishes the sounds of the TV. He only wants to see the images of mourning, the mourning that is their gift, their present. He doesn't need dishonest words, French words!

Who, what adolescent boys, scheming, numbed, hesitant, feverish, and finally enraged, clutching their weapons, which ones pulled the trigger, didn't pull the trigger, thought they were rendering justice when they first asked Tahar, in his car, ready to drive off:

"Are you Tahar Djaout?"

Tahar lowered the window, smiled vaguely but sincerely (one of the killers sees the smile again, not even a hesitant smile and not out of mere politeness at all; no, a real smile).

"Are you Tahar Djaout?" the man repeats.

And Tahar begins his sentence:

"What do you want from me?"

Or, to be more precise, what he answered was:

"Yes, what do you want from me?"

(And so he said 'yes' in good faith, calmly, and still smiling!...
He said 'yes,' and might as well have said:

"Yes, shoot!"
"Yes, kill me!"
"Yes, I'm here to be sacrificed!"
"Yes, I offer myself because of my writing!"
He said: "Yes.")

The one who translated the mother's Berber laments, he does nothing other than turn over and relive the last minute of this Tahar, as his hand was lowering the window, the other hand on the steering wheel, and the shadow of the fading smile.

The one who questioned him soliloquizes in the darkness of the room. He gets up, turns off the TV, curses the TV of the French. He spits on the floor. He, this first one, was not the one who shot him twice in the head; it's his colleague who now stares at him harshly:

"Calm down! They'll come tomorrow or maybe even tonight, to take us back up with them!..."

The weapons have disappeared. They shave this morning. They'll dress like middle class men, sons of the middle class. They're young; they think they're handsome. They're waiting to join the underground again. Others will replace them here. Two have already inherited their guns.

Who, what murderers completed their course, their mission ordered by the emir in the mountains who waits to congratulate them, what armed men ran, walked, to Tahar's house to hail him—he, smiling at them—to shoot him in the head, then leave his collapsed body on the ground, and flee in the victim's car?

A quarter of an hour later, the vehicle abandoned, they return here to this first shelter. They change their faces, clothes, and their appearance. The dreamer, even after he turns off the TV, ends up by saying in the dark:

"You see, if it was me falling, there, in the village, my old lady would cry just like Tahar's! Only..."

"Only what?" the other asks, exasperated.

"Only, the TV of the Christians or of these bastards here wouldn't go out of their way for my mother, that's for sure!"

They stop talking and wait in the darkness of the room.

Reporting on the death of Tahar Djaout continues. A journalist, faced with Kenza's gaze, asks her:

"What do you want to do when you grow up?"

And Kenza with shining eyes:

"I want to write! Write, like my father!"

REMORSE BY THE NAME OF AMIROUCHE

Now comes the time of the cutthroats! Comes? No, sadly, that bloody time was here already, slipped by us during yesterday's war, and we didn't know it. And we didn't know it until after 1962: even then, through scraps of vague avowals, half–suggested confidences.

One fine day, I read the account of the journalist Yves Courrière, published in 1970 and, as we soon found out, inspired by Krim Belkacem—who, it seems, opened his heart at the time that he was moving irreversibly to oppose Boumediene's power, which was growing stronger. For having backed (and even directly contributed to) the era of liquidations himself, he no doubt felt the need to speak to a neutral witness.

I read the "blue-itis" episode, a danger Colonel Amirouche ran into, when in 1957 he became the leader of the Kabylian underground. Amirouche had commented on the assassination of Abane, arguing that this measure had come too late! Had Abane himself not said at the Soummam Congress in Tunis that, because he had criticized Amirouche and Mohamedi Saïd on their summary methods with the population (especially the sinister episode of Melouza), Amirouche had been tempted to take revenge by suppressing him! The warlord, in his brutality, confronted with the political leader who tries to surmount personal conflicts with a strategy, a thought, an ideal to be constructed as collective action! It was Abane's Utopia, which then was adopted by several other fighters, who would also pay for this idealism with their lives. Questionable deaths, said to have been suffered "on the field of honor!"

The "blue-itis" then.

The struggle is no longer between two camps, for French Algeria or for an Algeria that is finally independent. The "Battle of Algiers" ends with the arrest of Yacef Saadi and the death of Ali la Pointe in September and October of 1957. The scene is suddenly darkened by the "blue overalls" of Captain Léger (veteran of the French Resistance, then of Vietnam, specialist of the secret war, double- and triple-faced, he will cause the Kabylian underground heavy losses!).

Former collaborators of Yacef Saadi—now "reeducated", some through torture, others without being pressured, some openly compromised, but still others (Guendriche, Hani, "Ourdia" the darkhaired one) having been double agents in the capital as early as the summer of '57—these former collaborators work for several months under the leadership of Léger on a successful operation against a section of the administrative staff of Amirouche's District III, in January '58.

Then comes the period of suspicion, of confusion, of betrayal: the Kabylian underground has tried to bring urban terrorism back to the capital; in less than four months comes disgraceful failure. Henceforth the underground, mountain people and farmers, will show a marked mistrust of the urban recruits who have volunteered in huge numbers following the student strike of '56; these young people are unprepared, burdened by their good will, their faith...and by whatever else, their knowledge (diplomas from the French school, even modest ones!). With their knowledge of French, and sometimes their comfortable social status, why would these young people become involved in the "revolution," the *djounouds*, the resistance workers, wonder? They find them suspect!

The conspiracy of Hani and Guendriche, guided by Captain Léger, was in fact very real. Léger, this time on the managerial staff of General Salan's B.E.L. (Bureau d'Études et de Liaison), decides to perfect the trap, to make it even more evil. A whole covert program: "Let terrorism turn against itself!" he explains.

A sophisticated process: if they're up against Nationalist agents who "hold out", who cannot be "re-educated," who are unwavering even after many seductive interviews, well then, let's turn their devotion to their organization against itself, increasing the suspiciousness already present up in the mountains.

Thus there is poor "Roza," a young activist whom Léger, during the interrogations, lets see some letters, supposedly signed by an underground leader, some notes prepared using carefully collected information. Eventually they let the young girl go home, though she must still report regularly for control purposes. A few days later, she flees to the mountains, to the underground, thinking she will find refuge!

But despite herself, she becomes a suspect to her own people. Two or three other agents, not as overtly but similarly in spite of themselves, find themselves roughly interrogated like "Roza." Amirouche has inquisitors in his entourage who are expert in these matters. Their procedures of torture are more rudimentary, but just as effective, as the "hell" in the villas of Algiers.

Once unleashed, the process gathers speed. Two or three innocents, mistakenly persecuted, will give the names they thought they'd intercepted from Léger. They are reliable activists, who happened to be experienced administrative staff and... with degrees, French-speaking! No doubt about it, agents from France!

The hunt is on: death to the students who have joined up in massive numbers, to the intellectuals coming from the cities to fuse their revolutionary spirit with that of the "peasant masses," to the youth that speak and write French, to so many others.... From the spring of '58 to March '59 (when Amirouche dies in battle), the great purge, orchestrated by him and his henchmen and refined to the point of obsession, runs rampant. The dreaded Colonel even coaches the other districts in his methods of "purification."

The leaders of the Aurès will not accept this, will see the dangerous paranoia of Amirouche. The leadership of District IV, close to Algiers—though filled with a true spirit of democracy reigned there among its political leaders—wavers for a moment. Then recovers.

The result of the "purification": two thousand, they say, maybe three thousand young people—ages sixteen to twenty-five—including women obviously!

They spoke and wrote French. They had therefore drunk the sap of "the French mind-set" from childhood on. They were suspected of talking at the first interrogation, of making deals with their captors. Yes, because by nature, because of their new language, they were already "traitors." Traitors in spite of their youthful membership, in spite of their rush join the underground, wanting to live among the peasants, suddenly happy!...Traitors without knowing it in short: what was certain is that at the first sign of danger they would talk, they would desert! Yes, crush the all too vulnerable branches of trees that must stand tall.

And Amirouche, with his vengeful finger (to avenge what, though?), giving orders once, ten times, to cut their throats, kill the young!

Killers of intellectuals—of young people glad to be writing, dissemi-
nating knowledge, who see themselves as teachers. There they are,
these murderers, around Amirouche (who now rests in the Carré des
Martyrs in El-Alia in Algiers). They rise up, determined, turning their
own children into Aïd's sheep for the great sacrificial celebration of
Abraham, feeling none of the Biblical prophet's anguish, expecting
no interruption whatsoever in the divine clemency. No, they rush at
the throats of these young heroes, wading in blood, then wiping the
knife with the terrifying good conscience of the man in the herd,
blindly obeying the obtuse leader.

Amirouche and the two thousand, three thousand throats he slit!

*A young cousin of my mother's whom I remember, just before 1954.
Young and frail, the pride and joy of his mother, a pious and refined
matron, he her only son.*

*In 1956 I learned that he had become an assistant cameraman with
the very new television of Algiers. While his mother was preparing his
engagement celebration, he "went up to the mountains"—that's what they
said when people left to join the* maquis—*part of a whole, well-con-
structed and homogeneous team that joined the closest Kabylian section
of the* maquis *as an "information department."*

*His mother wept, consoled herself with gentle patriotic pride: her son
would not yet get married but already he was a hero!...*

*He was one of Amirouche's victims; in all likelihood he, too, had his
throat slit. When his mother was dying she was still convinced that her
only son had been killed in battle.*

*So it went for the majority of families in 1962, when two thousand
educated and French-speaking young people did not come back; two or
three thousand who were sacrificed on the initiative of the French Services
and through the blind fury of Amirouche.*

Ferhat Abbas, who in 1958 was following the internal divisions, spoke several times with bitterness of the "anti-intellectualism" of these warlords. Abane's fears during his last months in Tunis were confirmed.

Less than forty years later, they are killing journalists, doctors, teachers, female professors and nurses, they are killing anyone with "degrees" even though they have no power, don't seek to protect themselves—don't give that any thought—while living in working class neighborhoods, while...

Kill the just, because the unjust are behind closed doors, find shelter, and continue to reap their profits. Target the one who speaks, who says "I," who expresses an opinion; who thinks he is defending democracy. Kill the one who is on the path: the path of many languages, many lifestyles, the one who stays on the fringe, who walks, unconcerned about himself or each day invents his own truth.

Only now, having spilled a tiny bit of my inconsolable loathing, am I able to move forward to the body, the heart, the face, and the smile of Youssef Sebti.

Youssef, the poet whose throat was slit, two days after Christmas 1993, near Algiers.

PROCESSION 3 (continued)

3

Soon the poet will reach the end of his fiftieth year. He is still frail, his markedly sharp face, the same fine goatee, his enormous eyes widened by fever—at times lit up with a streak of tenderness.... The young man he was is still there somewhere, with that charm of before, the intensified sensitivity still there. His thinking has been made more rigorous by the eternal fight against bureaucratic sterility, against...new monsters that have suddenly appeared. Sometimes Sebti uses words excessively, Sebti the friend of simple people, of unknown people on the road, and of enthusiastic students who revere him, at least the purest among them who are like him, who from him expect...

Knowledge? Not only that. He gives courses in agrarian sociology in clear, nervous, and precise Arabic; only recently did this become the language of his poetry—a vehement, grating, sometimes contentious use of words.

Youssef is tender; hard and tender—hard as a diamond, a cracked diamond, and transparent rather than tender. A protected youth, as during the time twenty years earlier of the "gang of Sénac," when many young people, confident and passionate about poetry, would randomly celebrate Algerian poetry and the rural revolution!...A sheltered youth, but one in which the suffering persists of a child born in the middle of the war in Eastern Algeria who grows up in the "forbidden zone":

201

I shed tears for the retreating summer
I think of old age
of death
that will devour me
long before
the spring returns.

It was the early sixties; he was thirty years old and beginning to teach sociology at the Institute of Agronomy of El-Harrach.

Twenty years later. Lately he has begun to lose his temper, sometimes with his colleagues or even with his friends; he harbors a strange sarcasm against the "franciscan" (as he rather harshly calls French-speaking intellectuals, as if he smelled a caste spirit among some of them). He continues to be at the center of danger; he notices the least little crack, he anticipates the muted explosion, he condemns the use of French "which is not the language of civilization" but merely chitchat and empty words. Sometimes he calls certain people "French-speaking mutants"; he has no qualms about attacking this or that well-known writer.

Sebti is a poet first, he is incorruptible, and beneath his vulnerable physical appearance, he seeks neither praise nor success. And for that alone he is suspect. He has the fire of a Saint-Just, and shrewder Arabic-speaking writers know how to use his unremitting hard work, his patience (he would be named secretary of a cultural association, put in the shadow of el-Djahiz, the great ironist of the classical Arabic period.

"Youssef Sebti," one of his earliest women friends, also a sociologist, told me, "Youssef would speak, would get so vehement.... I always felt he was like a candle—fragile, of course, and constantly self-consuming! He was burning himself out! He was exhausting himself, because of his candor."

Suddenly, I added:

"Because of loneliness?"

"Yes," she agreed, "loneliness, too!"

He is first and foremost a poet. ("Poetry is not just words. It is a form of being..." he used to say.) In '92, '93, he has friends and enemies. However, nobody would have thought he might be murdered.... Just say it out loud, friends: what would be the point of killing a poet?

They finished him off during the night. A long night, beneath the painting (a large reproduction) of Goya's *Executions on the Third of May*. On the wall, then, the members of the firing squad never stop shooting; the victims on the wall, their arms raised, with bewildered faces, never stop being blown away.

On that night of Monday, the 27th of December, forty-eight hours after Christmas, they came, three young strangers, into the little house (during the time of the French, it had been the house of the local policeman; his neighbors on the second floor, Sebti downstairs). He was sleeping. In the din, in the wordless struggle, they were grunting like wild animals, surrounded him as his large eyes opened; perhaps he was still asleep, telling himself slowly: "This is a nightmare from which I'll soon wake up," or mumbling: "This is a poem in action, composing and undoing itself, it's a dark poem"; perhaps he kept repeating as in one of his last texts: "Of these here, who is the devil, who is the angel, or the angel playing the devil, and vice versa...." They continued to harass him, waving their knives, trying to create terror in his childlike eyes (not an ounce), dread (not a breath), wishing he would beg for mercy at least, while Youssef's eyes—widened, shining with life—are watching:

"The messengers have come at last, but messengers of what, of what hatred or what betrayal, what contempt, what unalterable and permanent madness.... I am, I remain, the three of you are helping me to assume

the role I have sought since my birth, I am the immolated one, I am the
necessary and fatal sacrifice, my name is no longer Youssef but Ismaël, not
replaced at the moment of sacrifice, or maybe I am Youssef but forever at
the bottom of the well or truly thrown to the wolves by his brothers and
mangled, eternally mangled!...

You are immobilizing me and I stretch my neck out to you, were you
to free me right now I would offer you my throat as well as my invincible
revolt! You have come at last!..."

One of the three assailants spat out a few sentences:

"And so you tell your students over and over again, and brag
about it, that you don't believe in God, that you don't believe in His
Prophet. You announce this in your classes, you brag about it, you're
nothing but a heretic!"

And Sebti would almost smile as he remembers his anathemas in
such beautiful Arabic: indeed, his poetry and his truth, together! The
beauty of the anathema, making young minds, girls and boys, feel it,
and may it be in the footsteps of al-Mutanabbi or Abou al-Ala al-
Maari, the great audacious poets of our Arabic heritage!

A brief second in which Youssef Sebti floats in the past oceans of
great poetry!

Then the second executioner:

"And so we will impose the sentence!"

Sebti's enormous eyes stare at the blade in his executioner's hand.
The beginning of a long-ago poem, at least twenty years old: so he
had the foreboding then of this December night:

I was born in hell
I have lived in hell
And hell was born in me!
Hell and Madness: the title of the collection had frightened the

bureaucrats of the national publishing houses: it lay in a drawer for more than ten years.

Suddenly Youssef, sliding out of bed, escapes from the strangers; he struggles, he tries to get to the door. Turmoil and fierce fighting in the room: furniture is overturned, the racket of the struggle. The two killers are surprised by this turnaround, the third one had gone out for just a moment to be on the lookout.... But perhaps they're only pretending to let him have some hope of escape before they flatten him on the bed with one blow—with just his dagger in his right hand, the most determined one cuts his throat: Youssef's eyes stay wide open for the duration of the interminable death rattle.

At what time during the night or just before dawn did he expire? Terrified neighbors got up in the dark and hid behind their doors; through the blinds they saw, much later, shadows slip away through the vast abandoned garden.

They kept on watching. The neighbors didn't go back to sleep.

Youssef had been their friend for a long time; benefactor and counselor to some of their teenagers. They are afraid. They're trembling when morning comes. They hide. When the body is discovered—the door had been left open, besides—they don't want to testify. They have seen nothing, heard nothing. They fear vengeance, one night, killers; resistance workers, that is, from the mountain nearby.

They, the neighbors, will not go to mourn the one who was their friend yesterday; they will not go to the cemetery. They won't say a word to the students who will certainly come flocking...

They know nothing—nothing about nothing—these neighbors!

In the evening of that same Monday the 27th of December, a young woman, Naïma, a friend of Youssef's, remembers and then writes:

"On this Monday the 27th of December, the weather was beautiful. Algiers was radiant with its finest colors. In the car that took us to the Place des Martyrs, we were making endless plans, we were talking about the future. I now hold it against you that you sneaked away from me right afterwards, at eleven at night to your retreat. There were three of them and only one of you. They were armed and your only parry was your very frail gaze, your hands as light as olive branches. The olive tree of El-Milia, the land of your birth that will never be your shroud."

A few days after the funeral, this letter from a living person to an assassinated one is answered by a letter, dated fifteen months earlier, which Sebti had addressed to another dead man—I was going to say to the first dead one in this burdensome procession here—to Boudiaf:

"Will you read this letter, you whom they took from behind by surprise, while you were unraveling the pages of our national destiny once again?

I forgot to tell you, dear Mohammed Boudiaf. That's because the surprise caused by your precipitous, yet foreseeable departure, left me hanging. Suspended. Tense...

Well then, let's be like ice and see that death is only a passage.

And in the case of dying—that is to say of coming apart into a host of fragments bordering on total chaos—it is putting your foot in the stirrups of the absolute or at the very least of another unity, that is to say of another life or another way of being...

I admit to you that I felt some enchantment once I had gotten over my initial shock. I am content, in the way a son is content whose deceased father has left him a burnoose, a rifle, and whatever else.

You have left us your scrupulousness and the exercise of power would neither have tarnished nor dirtied you. Nor blackened you...

They have killed you in the grandeur of the generosity that was yours. With treachery, it is true, but neatly."

The very phrase can be applied to you as well: "They have killed you in the grandeur of the generosity that was yours." Yes.... They have killed you "neatly": oh yes!

Three or four days prior to this sinister night, at the Institute of Agronomy where, for your own pleasure and that of a few of your most loyal students, you were running a writing workshop, you went up to a young girl—perhaps the student you most believed in—and, with your very gentle smile though with a hint of irony, you handed her a few sheets of paper:

"Here, I'm giving you back your last poems! I've already told you everything I like about them!...But they shouldn't stay at my place!"

You hesitated; the young girl, taking her pages back, had a questioning look, didn't know in fact how to interpret this smile of the professor—like a sudden melancholy.... You added:

"If they come to kill me one of these days, I want my things to be in order."

Suddenly you turned your back on her. You left the young girl standing there, her heart pounding.

4

On Thursday the 1st of December 1994, Saïd Mekbel's daily column appeared in the *Matin*. The master of political humor targets a leader of the future opposition, whom he attacks but, more than the object of the polemic itself, it is, as so often with Mekbel, the deadly commentary that gives it flavor:

"Mehri declared: 'Presidential elections are a false solution!' Is he right? Would it not have been better for him to say: 'Presidential elections are the wrong solution'?"

And Mekbel, no dummy, hit the nail on the head. (The title of his column is *"Mesmar Djha,"* that is to say "the nail" hit by the popular Algerian hero, an expert with words of mockery: Djha!) A false solution and a wrong solution are not, he explains, the same things at all: "A false solution is a solution that has nothing to do with the problem posed. While a wrong solution does not solve the problem at hand," Mekbel maintains with that taste for precision he seems to have gotten from his scientific training. Then he concludes, concealing his bitterness a little: "All to say that the end of our tunnel will start to be visible when the true problem has been ascertained!"

The next day is Friday, the day set aside for Islamic prayer and, for the past twenty years now, the official weekend in Algeria. It is also a day without newspapers.

I can very well imagine that Saïd Mekbel that day did not leave his little villa on the outskirts of Algiers, where he lives. The house of a civil servant, which he occupies through his position as a manager of the National Gas and Electric Company, where he has made almost his entire career: more than a hobby, journalism is his sin, his drug, and his oxygen!...

For the past few months he has been living there alone: his wife, who is French, and his two boys, both students, could no longer—almost two years now—deal with the death threats Saïd repeatedly receives, by mail and by phone. He urged them to leave, took them to the airport, went back to lock himself in his lair where he has installed and controls safety devices with maniacal precision.

Furthermore, he is thereafter a full time journalist. He assumes the direction of the newspaper, working with the team of young people who revere him for his warmth, his generosity, and his predilection for half-gentle banter.

Every morning when he goes to the paper, and every evening when he comes home, it is this round trip that poses the most likely risk of being targeted and attacked.

This Friday, then, he must not have left his house; he would have spoken on the phone with his family, then perhaps with his friends in Algiers. Toward the end of the day, after having looked after his dogs and stilled his desire to go out for a while—in the neighborhood, in the village: it is such a beautiful day, the December light, the first departures of flocks of swifts in the sky, what else, an intangible nostalgia or the sweetness of solitude, he doesn't know—he sat down at his table and began to write his next column.

He doesn't understand. Usually, he is concise from the very start; brevity and intensity come to him right away, and now.... This must not be a good day. He writes, he writes, and decidedly finds this "column" a bit long; yes, really too long! That is not his ordinary trademark. A bit more and he'd call himself chatty. Something he really doesn't like (he's always felt that chatter and verbosity have destroyed this country, have brought it out of its innate culture!). His text is, in fact, original in its rhythm and reasoning. But it is as if he wanted to double its length in the next publication! As if suddenly he had so very much to say...but why?

He doesn't finish the column. Not that he is unhappy with it, no, but he feels his regular habits have been upset. Oh well, he won't hand the article in tomorrow, he'll wait for the day after!

On Saturday the 3rd of December he goes to work, leaving the unfinished text on his desk.

On the afternoon of the same day, a major demonstration by

many French and emigrant associations in solidarity with Algeria is announced in Paris...

"That will do our hearts good!" someone says in the group crowding into the director's office at the *Matin*.

A little after twelve, Mekbel decides to have lunch with two young co-workers at the small restaurant next to the office.

Soon after, two young strangers come to Saïd Mekbel's table and, one after the other, put two bullets in his head. He is the twenty-seventh journalist to be assassinated since the 12th of May '93 when Tahar Djaout was the first victim.

On the small desk, Saïd's last questions lie waiting:

"I would like to know," he had begun, not thinking this was the day before his death, "who is going to kill me? But is that what I would like to know first and foremost? Because there are other questions, perhaps more important ones. For example, how will I be killed and why are they going to kill me? When are they going to kill me?

"I notice I'm not using the word assassinate. Why? No doubt because, whether assassinating or killing, the result is the same: in either case, I end up at the bottom of the same hole in the ground."

Thus, on this last Friday, Saïd lets his pen run as it follows his inner dialogue.... What I like in this man of the pen—whom I met only once, spending a whole afternoon at his house with his family: laughing, silent, of a tenderness he could not hide beneath his apparent timidity—what characterizes him, in this procession of which he is the last member, is his love of words, words in any language—French, Arabic and Berber words, his penchant for word play, subtle and sometimes facile, but pure play, oh yes, truly pure play, especially if he had lived somewhere other than Algeria! Or precisely because he lived in Algeria, because he recognized himself in the legendary character of this land, with his dreaded humor: Djha, the new Djha, the falsely naïve one, and beyond desperate, and actually laughing because of that and making others laugh!

And I come back to his patient curiosity, moving along step by step, feeding one question after the other—as if he were savoring each stop along the path of his quest, albeit with its funereal coloring:

"To kill or to assassinate? I'll go for kill. It's short, quick, a movement in two beats like bang-bang. While assassinate is complicated, is looking for difficulties, calling for the butcher's knife, several movements laden with hatred and cruelty. Then, in addition, if you add 'savagely assassinated' or 'most cowardly and savagely,' no.

"In the final analysis, I prefer kill, it should hurt less. Assassinate is made for the reader, for his imagination. Kill is for the victim."

Saïd Mekbel was killed on the 3rd of December in a small restaurant in Algiers where he was having lunch with his colleagues. We heard about it a few hours later, on that sunny Saturday during the march from the Place de la République to the Place de la Nation in Paris.

"The victim is alone, the assassins many and varied.... Sometimes I very much feel like meeting the assassins and above all the men behind them...The victim never knows when he is going to be killed: the assassins, on the other hand, know when do they are going to act. What are their reactions? When they choose the way in which they're going to operate? Before, during, and after the assassination? What part of their action will stay with them?"

Thus, on the 3rd of December, while we are dispersing in Paris, while some begin to suffer again from that uncomfortable pain of knowing too much, not knowing the new "victim"—but knowing that he was "alone" in that last moment, and because we are elsewhere, safe and sound, safe and sick, alive.... Saïd's voice remains fiery, audible and fiery above his worktable. Of course, you wanted your text—your last "nail of Djha"—to be unfinished, hanging suspended in air, because suddenly the wall, the low wall, the prison in front of you was already vanishing, but your voice not at all, nor your laughter, nor your questioning that would harry us...

Since his first column, on the 23rd of September, 1963, for the relaunched *Alger républicain*, Saïd, then barely twenty-two years old, had pursued with ironic curiosity and masked anguish (he supposedly managed to tame that old anguish with each one of his "nails"), his questioning about others, the unknown, the assassins: "What of their action will stay with them?"

He would draw them a little longer, with a rapid charcoal line, or India ink meant not to dry up; a little longer, he would disarm them with his innocent smile or with his pen, hopping around in daily mockery this time:

"My father isn't upbeat enough.... My sister Yasmina is fourteen years old.... Then there's my aunt Zouina who predicted.... My mother blames my father's ill health on the Democrats and the Republicans, with their trivial preoccupations!..."

And in the last column published while he was alive, he concluded, cushioning his sadness:

"While we wait, our country is sick with its Republic and its Democracy. Very sick!"

In Bejaia, on the 6th of December, '94, as in Oran on the previous 16th of March for Abdelkader Alloula, an entire city came out, women and men of all walks of life, to hold a princely funeral for one of its finest sons. After the "prayer for the dead" had been read, the funeral oration was pronounced by Omar Belhouchet, the director of *El-Watan*.

As they walked to the cemetery above the immense bay, his many colleagues repeated these two improvised lines of verse over and over again:

> *Sahafiyin hr'ar*
> *Ma ya' Quablouch el 'ar!*

> *Journalists, the brave ones,*
> *Will never accept evil!*

The list of journalist victims—"killed" rather than "assassinated"—Mekbel would say with a mischievous glint in his eye—has risen above forty in the course of these past six months, in this country "sick with its Republic and its Democracy."

IV
Writing the White of Algeria

"Obliteration, imprisonment, repression, isolation—
so many negatives have assailed this harsh, dense land
since the beginning, its black destiny, whose feminine side
seems only to have aggravated the widespread cruelty.

Yes, so vast the Algerian prison!

JACQUES BERQUE
letter to AD., June 2, 1995
(five days before his death)

I

Others speak of Algeria, describe it, question it; they try, they think, to illuminate its path. What path?

Half of the land of Algeria has just been seized by moving, terrifying and sometimes hideous shadows.... It is no longer just the night of women separated, isolated, exploited as mere child-bearers—for generations on end!

What path, that is to say what future?

Others know, or ask themselves.... Still others, certain compatriots like myself, listen for the news every worried morning, sometimes trembling, pierced by exile.

Others write "about" Algeria, its prolific misfortune, how its monsters returned.

All I do in these pages is spend time with a few friends. I've become closer to them, as well as to the irreversible frontier that tries to separate me from them.... As I write, a few tears have finally fallen on my cheeks: tears that are suddenly made tender because through them I so clearly see the half-smile of M'Hamed Boukhobza (*"tafla,"* he would say when speaking of me, a mutual friend told me—"the little one?" I had to translate, surprised); because I gaze at the exact image of Kader walking through the streets of Oran—his tall bearing, his calm and serene face, his radiant gaze, his indulgent or secret laughter—I dance again with Mahfoud Boucebci, whose look is self-tormenting in flashes...

I am nearer to the ones I love; they still live for me. I regret never having known how to admit my affection for them; I suffer from having at one instance caused Kader pain, Kader with his inexhaustible goodness and patience!

It saddens me that I did not cancel a trip in order to stay in Paris to have chatted one last evening with Mahfoud—I didn't know, I didn't dream that they were going to leave one day, would vanish, would fade away.

I write and I dry a few tears. I don't believe in their deaths: for me, their deaths are works–in–progress.

Others speak of their beloved Algeria, a place they know and visit. For me, thanks to these few friends lying here in this text—and a few colleagues, vanished too soon— some of them still writing on their last day: poems, an article, a page of a novel that would remain unfinished—persistent, I resuscitate them or imagine doing so.

Yes, so many others speak of Algeria fervently or with anger. Directing myself to my departed ones and comforted by them, I dream of it.

2

Suddenly, I'm counting. How many writers (poets, essayists, novelists) in the French language—it could just as well be Arabic or Berber, no matter—will find each other as they inevitably approach death, pen or writing brush in hand, and then succumb to it.

Every writer, like any other person, educated or illiterate, is mortal. Why, on Algerian land and in the year '95 specifically, am I so obsessed by the coupling of death—that black and thoroughbred mount—and writing?

In solidarity with circumstances? No. As a way to defend myself now—my friends and colleagues, are you my oracles, you who barely turn around for a smile, are you calling me? Perhaps not.

The journalist writing in Algeria as in Egypt, in Central America or elsewhere, is exposed to bullets, to assassination attempts. Certainly the writer, whether he wants to be a journalist, or merely a witness, in his crisis-ridden country, or is freed to flee, is not specifically Algerian.

If, in an attempt to tell the sometimes anecdotal circumstances of the accident, of the assassination attempt or the suicidal vertigo, I have called this interrogative journey "the unfinished death," it is without a doubt—was that a first intuition that began to gnaw at me?—because written literature throughout this century, starting both with the publication of *Nedjma* by Kateb Yacine in 1956 and in January '60, when Camus, not yet fifty, leaves a kind of fraternal void (because of the unfinished status of what was going to be his "great Algerian novel")—because this literature lived its beginnings, let's say its first soaring even, in agony. Barely thirty years later, it knows collapse, with the evidence more and more obvious.

Writing in Algeria, our own extinction? In spite of it, certainly, and sometimes beside it? Beside it to celebrate weddings, laughter, bedazzlement—the same as a steady sun. Perhaps the same (I perceive the metaphor because I am a woman) as writing in the beginning, writing the beginning (beginning of the self and of others, I mean of sisters, awakened grandmothers, little girls escaped on the road), writing the first steps of departure, the half-open doorway, the road suddenly lit up to the sky, the journey stretched to infinity, oh yes, writing this way would be like keeping a full moon, hovering and serene, over your head.

Protective moon: "*Badra,*" a first name that bodes well. Nights of the full moon are never shores of death but fountains of hope, messengers of love, thirst-quenching.

Such itineraries promise nocturnal dances, bacchanals of innocence for adolescent scribes, for thieves of writing, for lively runaways, for opulent ladies carrying the secret letters of the cherished alphabet in their closed hands.

Writing in Algeria, would that be this unfinished death that becomes tumultuous: the desert approaching, lost caravan moving across a blinding present? Would that be the legacy Isabelle Eberhardt is supposed to have foreseen, in a flash, in the last seconds of her delicate life, just before the roaring waters surrounded her? Isabelle, mystical and marginal, a Muslim and a free woman, who spoke Russian and Arabic but wrote in French.

At the other end of the century, Josie, my older sister, flew across the threshold of her window and her last look caressed the terraces of El-Biar, which a few months earlier had been purified by the blood of young rebels by the hundreds.

Two travelers, having come to Algeria to settle, marvel, suffer, write. Two adopted women immediately adopting the silence and the fever of all whom they meet and know to be fettered.

Death truly a work–in–progress? For me today, if I persist in going on, it is rather death to be tamed—in an Algerian night that is no longer colonial.

In this procession, which I have traced in stages, some may reproach me for having neglected Arabic writers (the young poet Houhou from Constantine, who died in the Resistance, as well as the author of the national anthem, Moufdy Zacharia, who died later in exile).

And shall I mention, in Spanish—nearest to us after all among our European hybrids—the woman who speaks of "hitting the white," that is to say of target shooting, shall I mention my white as well? The richest of colors and the least deceiving, that round pool of language in me, in us—the language of the Other, having become tunic, veil or armor for some, or more rarely, skin!

Upstream from this movement, the permanence of the bastion language so very much older, unwritten for so long, which this death also straddles: at the century's beginning two poets die, both Mohand—Mohand or Lhocine, Cheikh of Takka, and Mohand or Mhand, the thief—the holy visionary of the metal of language and the vagabond bard, drunk on wine, women, and bitterness.

Receding further, to one already dead twenty years before these two, the greatest Arabic writer and poet of Algeria—in the last century and even in this century—the emir Abdelkader el-Djazaïri, the inspired author of the *Livre des haltes (Kitab el-Mawaqef)*.

An exemplary trio for the inauguration of Algerian literature today, which will see its own face crushed in blood and hatred in this final decade.

<u>3</u>

Two paternal bodies transported—moved in spite of their secular sleep:

one, Saint Augustine, expelled, and the other the emir Abdelkader, brought back. Land of coming and going; of the coming and going of the dead, the remains, the bones; homeland where they never stop negotiating corpses—and like today, alas, less their work, their words, their preserved light than what remains of the body: a skeleton, a nail, a hair, some relic that will allow for statues to be erected, for the flow of speeches, for any ceremony at all.

Land of the vanished fathers, always absent and who can now be invoked ad nauseam, masked, betrayed, who can be forgotten! From here on in, orphaned sons abound, overshadowed, fleeing behind their faces, their felonies, their boastfulness, with the cruelty of enraged jackals! Yes, certainly, sons without fathers, each one forever fearing the resuscitated gaze of the latter should he come back by some misfortune, alive, to weigh on them!

One fine day, they said—first in the time of Ben Bella—they would like to return the body of the great hero, the emir Abdelkader, to his native soil. In the end they did it—this was in the time of Boumediene: ceremonies, photographs and reporting, speeches; and a wretched statuette placed in a narrow intersection of the city center.

It is not true: Abdelkader's body did not really come back!

They said that it was normal for the hero of Algerian independence to rest at last in the land of his ancestors, now that the country was liberated. It isn't true. A mere illusion: he does not rest and if he is really there, I know, I am sure of it, he is turning over and over in his grave.

In his final years, he wished to sleep in the mosque of the Omeyyads of Damascus where his master, Ibn Arabi, lies in bliss… Abdelkader, dead in serenity in Damascus!

In the year 1966, they were in no hurry to publish the poems of Abdelkader, to sing them, teach them, remember the spiritual message of his last meditations, and at the same time to study his war strategies, the technique of his mobility, his courage alone against all!... No. Schools will be opened everywhere in the young and new Algeria, universities will multiply: but no place will yet be found for the creative beauty, the intelligence, and the wisdom of Abdelkader!

Only his name, or at least his first name, was formally confiscated and transported. And then, his body!

Boumediene, second president of the new State, follows without knowing it the example of Liutprand, the Lombard king.

In 732 AD, this most pious king looks toward Sardinia—where already two centuries earlier the body of the Church Father, Saint Augustine the Algerian, was transported, he who had been expelled to Cagliari by one of the Aryan Vandal kings at the end of the fifth century. Seeing the threat of the Muslims this time, arriving in Spain and approaching Sicily and Sardinia, Liutprand thus wants to preserve the body of the father of all Christians. Once Saint Augustine's relic was brought from Cagliari to Genoa, he sent an entourage of ambassadors, emissaries, and dignitaries to accompany the majestic procession that was to solemnly transport the author of *The City of God* to the capital of Liutprand: Pavia, where he remains today.

In the ensuing six centuries, monks, poets, and humble believers flock as pilgrims to the body of Saint Augustine (when Dante Aleghieri arrives, he bears witness to this and two lines of verse from his *Paradiso* will be inscribed on the façade of the San Pietro Church in Ciel d'Oro which holds the mausoleum). While at the same time, Augustine's thinking, his books, his admonishments, his diatribes, his flights of words also circulate, across the roads of the West, inhabiting many monasteries and places of writing and prayer!

In the year 1966, thinking to legitimatize his new power thereby, the leader of the Algerian State definitely wants to have the body of Abdelkader, then resting in Damascus.

Envoys are sent for the final negotiations, since the emir has left innumerable descendants and, early in the century, the only one of his grandsons who returned to Algeria to build a life and career, the emir Khaled, found himself shamefully hounded out of the country.

The family member who is authorized to decide in everyone's name resides in Damascus; he is a *Djazaïri*, a man of science and a cabinet member. He negotiates with the envoys of the Algerian president. He wants nothing for himself. He will not go to the ancestral land. But it is for him to agree that Abdelkader's body may leave the mosque of the Omeyyads and be brought back here.

Here? They describe to him the "people" who are waiting, the planned festivities, the statue commissioned in Italy, the ceremony.... Abdelkader's heir listens to it all; does not flinch. Ends by saying:

"My son. One of my sons is in your country!"

"In Algeria?" they are surprised.

"Yes."

"Where?"

"In one of your prisons; he's been there for more than a year!"

Complete surprise. Nobody knew. The president didn't know. One of the direct descendants of the great resister in the prisons of Algiers? Astonishment. But the only ones arrested were Communists or others of that same ilk—arrested to keep them from doing any harm.

"Exactly, my son is one such. He has been incarcerated for his ideas (they are not my ideas, but he is my son); he has been tortured!"

It's a mistake, a ghastly mistake, they say. It is true that the heir did not reveal himself as such, but only as an activist with a cause.

"Set my son free and you may return my grandfather to your country!"

It seems those were the terms he used: "You may return him to your country!"

That is why the old man, who will not leave his office in Damascus for the splendors of the Bay of Algiers, who has negotiated the freedom of his youngest son, smiles: he knows that returning just the bones of Abdelkader is pure show.

He knows that his grandfather still sleeps close to his master, Ibn Arabi, blissful and serene. He knows that here, on liberated soil, here, thanks to a million sacrificed lives, his grandfather's poems of earthly and divine love will certainly end up being circulated one day, making an immense circle, making music and a crown above the dunes, the wadis, and the snowy mountains! Only then will the body truly follow!

Abdelkader ibn Mahieddine el-Djazaïri probably still sleeps in Damascus...

With his statue standing in the middle of a busy intersection, his mausoleum in the Carré des Martyrs in El-Alia in Algiers, Abdelkader, if he has truly come back to this land where he was first a soldier, will be better able than I to make the list of those who write and who, like so many others, are persecuted, silenced, pushed to suicide, to suffocation, or—through the intermediary of desperate youth, transformed into paid killers—killed by a single blow.

In this account I have only mentioned a few of those who, from the shore or deep in the sea of writing, have fallen—obliterated, drowned and already forgotten, executed.

If, really back in Algiers, Abdelkader were to rise every night to wander, if the Emir—the only true prince of Algeria—were to start roaming every night, a ghost of the nineties, if the Emir, then, were to begin tenderly scrutinizing all those who had not had time to prepare themselves for their final exit, surely he would count more than twenty, no, forty, at least forty thousand of them!

He would shudder, he would be distraught. Writing, he would say, doesn't matter, but let God's creatures have the chance to meet their deaths on their own; let them "hit the white," aim at the white circle themselves for their salvation or their damnation.

Algerian white.

4

In Algeria today, following the serial murders of writers, journalists, and intellectuals, against which increased repression is the response—the only policy brandished against a religious fundamentalism that has decided to take power at any cost—faced with these convulsions that submerge my country in a nameless war, once again referred to as "events," in this return to violence and its anaesthetizing vocabulary, what is "white" (the white of dust, of sunless light, of dilution...) and why say so here?

I can only express my disquiet as a writer and as an Algerian woman through a reference to that color, or rather that non-color. "White acts on our soul like absolute silence," Kandinsky said. Through the reminder of abstract painting, I have here begun a discourse that has in some way swerved.

The edges of the rift have opened halfway, surely irreversibly so; they have carried off many intellectuals into the abyss, some of the most audacious ones, others among the most reserved, and all this in a random and bloody lottery. Such a chain of violence and its blind acceleration certainly emphasize the uselessness of words, but their necessity as well.

A word that would not at first be one of passion, that, while feeling around in the dark for the limits of its reach, would know its own frailty and even its inanity, if it really is too late.... But beneath the leaden sky where it unfolds, which it drives out to set the traps and ambiguities: for example, the fact that the monopolizing media of any intellectual resistance succeeds only in an increased jamming, the white zone of the projectors widening the desert...

For I have been haunted—even before these storms—by a long and lasting morbidity where Algerian culture is debated, the discourse secreting and stirring the latent ferments of discord—not only because of the obvious debasement of the political word, having very rapidly become hairsplitting, and of the socio-theoretical conclusion enclosed in its knowledge or its jargon—no.

It has often seemed to me that, in a culturally more and more fragmented Algeria (where tradition's sexual segregation has put the emphasis on locks and bolts), any word necessarily was impaired before it could even find for itself the trembling light of its very quest.... Yet, I am moved only by that particularity of a word faced with the imminence of disaster.

Writing and its urgency.

Writing to express Algeria vacillating and for which some are already preparing the white of the shroud.

Algerian literature—we must begin it with Apuleus in the second century and continue to Kateb Yacine and Mouloud Mammeri, passing Augustine, the emir Abdelkader, and Camus—has continuously been inscribed in a linguistic triangle:

—a language of rock and soil, the original one let's say, Libyco-Berber, which lost its alphabet momentarily except among the Tuareg;

—a second language, that of the prestigious exterior, of Mediterranean heritage—Eastern and Western—admittedly reserved for lettered minorities, which yesterday was Arabic, retained for a long time during colonialism in the shadow of the official French, what today becomes marginalized French when it is creative and critical, in which they claim hereafter to be only " a scientific and technical language" in the high schools and universities;

—the third partner in this triangle presents itself as the most exposed of the languages, the dominant one, the public one, the language of power: that of the harangues, but also the written one of the forensic scientists, the scribes, and the notaries. That was the role first assumed by Latin until Augustine, by classical Arabic in the Middle Ages, by Turkish which, during the time of the Kingdom of Algiers, took over the administrative and military domain (the State of Algiers abdicated before the French generals in the Turkish language!). After 1830, the French entered the scene in ceremonial colonial dress.

Today it is Arabic again, modern Arabic as it is called, which is taught to the young under the pompous guise of our "national language."

The institutionalized mediocrity of the educational system since 1962—despite a clear effort toward making the population literate: literacy has almost tripled in thirty years—was practiced on two levels: promoting the "national language" by officially restricting the living space of the other languages; then, in addition to this sterilizing monolingualism, the diglossia peculiar to Arabic (the structure's vertical variability that can give the child who is being educated a precious agility of mind) was handled badly by comparison with other Arab countries, by banishing a dialect that was vivid in its regional iridescence, subtle in the strength of its challenge and its dream.

Thus, the denial of an entire people's genius went hand in hand with the mistrust of a minority of French-language writers whose production, in spite of or for lack of anything better, continued in exile.

Jacques Berque, declaring in 1992 that "Islamism thinks of itself as material modernity, as it wholly refuses any intellectual bases," comes to Algeria and its linguistic choices: "Here is a situation," he says, "that exists in none of the other twenty Arab countries" also confronted with diglossia and the presence of one or two other languages. "One may say," he concludes, "that Algeria has shown a talent for creating a major problem out of something that began as an advantage!"

Writing and Algeria as territories. The desert of writing, "which from the blurred and broken white reconstructs the margin," said the poet André du Bouchet in 1986, in the house of Hölderlin, in Tübingen.

And the white of Algeria, "out of tune as if by snow?"

I seemed to have lingered over the ruins of a disintegrating knowledge, the pitiful failure of which should have led us to expect the first explosion, that of October '88, much sooner.

Six hundred corpses of youth laying in the sun. This bleeding white of the future had no right to any liturgical lamentation whatsoever in any of the three languages nor in the symphony of the three combined. Where then belonged poetry with its peaks and its abysses? The aphasia that seized us all was no longer condemnation; just a mask over a contorted face.

Kateb Yacine, whom I saw again in Brussels a month later, remained relentlessly silent. When he decided, a little later, to go into exile again to write, write his rage no doubt, leukemia—a white illness —took him.

The white of writing in a non-translated Algeria? For the moment, the Algeria of sorrow without writing; for the moment, an Algeria of writing-in-blood, alas!

How to withstand mourning for our friends, our colleagues, without first having sought to understand the why of yesterday's funerals, those of the Algerian utopia?

The white of a sullied dawn.

In the brilliance of this desert, in the safe harbor of writing in quest of a language beyond languages, by trying fiercely to obliterate all the furies of the collective self-devouring in oneself, finding "the word within" again that, alone, remains our fertile homeland.

Paris, April-July 1995

ALGERIAN WRITERS WHOSE DEATHS
ARE DESCRIBED IN THESE PAGES

Albert Camus: novelist, playwright, died January 4, 1960, aged 47, on the road of Villeblevin, Yonne (in a car accident).

Frantz Fanon: essayist, psychiatrist, died December 6, 1961, aged 36, near New York (from leukemia).

Mouloud Faraoun: novelist, died March 15, 1962, aged 49, in Algiers (assassinated by the O.A.S.).

Jean Amrouche: poet, died April 16, 1962, aged 56, in Paris (from cancer).

Jean Sénac: poet, died August 30, 1973, aged 47, in Algiers (assassinated).

Malek Haddad: poet, novelist, died June 2, 1976, aged 51, in Algiers (from cancer).

Mouloud Mammeri: novelist, died February 25, 1989, aged 71, on the road of Aïn-Defla, Algeria (in a car accident).

Kateb Yacine: novelist, playwright, died on October 28, 1989, aged 60, in Grenoble (from leukemia).

Anna Gréki: poet, died January 5, 1966, aged 35, in Algiers (during surgery).

Taos Amrouche: novelist and singer, died April 2, 1976, aged 63, in Paris (from cancer).

Josie Fanon: journalist, died July 13, 1989, aged 60, in El-Biar (Algiers) (by suicide).

Bachir Hadj Ali: poet, died May 10, 1991, aged 71, in Algiers (after a long illness).

Tahar Djaout: novelist and journalist, died June 3, 1993, aged 39, in Algiers (assassinated).

Youssef Sebti: poet, died December 27, 1993, aged 50, near Algiers (assassinated).

Saïd Mekbel: journalist, died December 3, 1994, aged 53, in Algiers (assassinated).

AND:

Mahfoud Boucebci: psychiatrist and author, died June 15, 1993, aged 54, in Birmandreis (Algiers) (assassinated).

M'Hamed Boukhobza: sociologist and author, died June 27, 1993, aged 55, in Algiers (assassinated).

Abdelkader Alloula: playwright, attacked March 11, 1993 in Oran, died in Paris on March 15, aged 55 (assassinated).

AND ALSO:

School principal (unnamed), died October 1994, aged 45, in Birmandreis (Algiers) (assassinated).

I would like to express my gratitude to those whose memories and research have allowed me to clarify certain scenes. Especially:

Ali Zaamoum: *Tamurt Imazighen,* Editions Rahma, Algiers, 1992.

Jean-Philippe Ould Aoudia: *L'Assassinat du Château-Royal,* Tiresias, 1992.

Djamila Amrane: *Des Algériennes dans la guerre,* Plon, Paris, 1993.

BIBLIOGRAPHY
(for the two chapters on the Algerian War):

Khalfa Mammeri: *Abane Ramdane* (biography), Editions Rahma, 1991.

Mohammed Lebdjaoui: *Vérités sur la Révolution algérienne*, Gallimard, 1970.

Mohammed Harbi: *Le F.L.N. Mirage et réalité*, Editions Jeune Afrique, 1980.

Benjamin Stora: *La Gangrène et l'Oubli*, Editions La Découverte, 1993.

Yves Courrière: *Le Temps des colonels*, Fayard, 1970.

Henri Jacquin: *La Guerre secrète en Algérie*, Olivier Orban, 1977.

I would like to thank a few friends who described scenes to me that I did not witness, namely:

Farida and Djaffar Lesbet
Abderahmane Tadjedine
Khelil Hamdane
Zohra Siagh
Alice Cherki
Laurence Bourdil
Nadjet Khedda

ASSIA DJEBAR, novelist, scholar, poet, and filmmaker, won Germany's premier literary prize, Le Prix de la Paix in 2000, the Neustadt Prize for Contributions to World Literature in 1996, the Yourcenar Prize in 1997. Djebar was educated in Algeria and France. Her other works translated into English include *So Vast the Prison* (1999, Seven Stories Press), *A Sister to Scheherazade* (1993), *Fantasia: An Algerian Cavalcade* (1993), and *Women of Algiers in their Apartment* (1992). Her first film, *La Nouba des Femmes de Mont Chenoua*, won the '79 Venice Biennale International Critics Prize. In 2000, she directed her musical drama *Filles de Ismael dans le vent et la tempête* at the Teatro di Roma. Djebar is a professor of French and Francophone Literature at New York University. She divides her time between Paris and New York.

DAVID KELLEY was among the world's most respected specialists of late 19th- and 20th-century French literature until his death, while translating *Algerian White* in 1999. He brought many contemporary poets to the attention of the English-speaking world, including Jean Tardieu.

MARJOLIJN DE JAGER translates literature and non-fiction works from the French and the Dutch. She won the ALTA Outstanding Literary Translation Award for her translation of Assia Djebar's *Women of Algiers in their Apartment* (University Press of Virginia, 1992).